Omori Sogen
The Art of a Zen Master

Omori Roshi and the ogane *(large temple bell) at Daihonzan Chozen-ji, Honolulu, 1982.*

Omori Sogen
The Art of a Zen Master

Hosokawa Dogen

Kegan Paul International
London and New York

First published in 1999 by Kegan Paul International
UK: P.O. Box 256, London WC1B 3SW, England
Tel: (0171) 580 5511 Fax: (0171) 436 0899
E-mail: books@keganpau.demon.co.uk
Internet: http://www.demon.co.uk/keganpaul/
USA: 562 West 113th Street, New York, NY, 10025, USA
Tel: (212) 666 1000 Fax: (212) 316 3100

Distributed by
John Wiley & Sons Ltd
Southern Cross Trading Estate
1 Oldlands Way, Bognor Regis
West Sussex, PO22 9SA, England
Tel: (01243) 779 777 Fax: (01243) 820 250

Columbia University Press
562 West 113th Street
New York, NY 10025. USA
Tel: (212) 666 1000 Fax: (212) 316 3100

Copyright © The Institute of Zen Studies 1999

All photographs copyright © 1995 by the Estate of Omori Sogen with the following exceptions: photograph of Omori Sogen facing the title page, copyright © 1982 by the Honolulu Star-Bulletin.

Printed in Great Britain

All rights reserved. No part of this book may be reprinted or reproduced or utilized in any form or by any electronic, mechanical or other means, now known or hereafter invented, including photocopying and recording, or in any information storage or retrieval system, without permission in writing from the publishers.

British Library Cataloguing in Publication Data

Dogen, Hosokawa
Omori Sogen : the art of a Zen master
1. Sogen, Omori 2. Zen Buddhists - Japan - Biography
I. Title
294.3'927'092
ISBN 0-7103-0588-5

Library of Congress Cataloging-in-Publication Data

Hosokawa, Dōgen
Omori Sogen, the art of a Zen master / by Hosokawa Dogen.
Includes bibliographical references and index.
ISBN 0-7103-0588-5 (alk. paper)
1. Ōmori, Sōgen. 1904 -   . 2. Spiritual life--Zen Buddhism.
3. Buddhism and arts. 4. Priests, Zen--Japan--Biography.
I. Title.
BQ976.M66H67   1997
294.3'927'092--dc21   97-25743
[B]   CIP

Dedicated to my parents

Contents

Acknowledgements	ix
Introduction	x
Part I - The Life of Omori Sogen	
Chapter 1 *Shugyo:* 1904–1934	3
Chapter 2 *Renma:* 1934–1945	39
Chapter 3 *Gogo no Shugyo:* 1945–1994	55
Part II - The Three Ways	
Chapter 4 Zen and *Budo*	101
Chapter 5 Practical Zen	115
Chapter 6 *Teisho:* The World of the Absolute Present	139
Chapter 7 Zen and the Fine Arts	153
Appendices	
Books by Omori Sogen	164
Endnotes	166
Index	171

Acknowledgments

Many people helped me to write this book, and I would like to thank them all. In particular, however, there are several I would like to acknowledge individually. Omori Roshi and Mrs. Omori not only kindly permitted me to use excerpts from his writings, but they also granted me interviews and consent to print irreplaceable photos. Mr. Trevor Leggett graciously took time from other writing projects to make careful editorial suggestions for Chapters 4, 5, and 6. In this effort, Mr. Leggett was assisted by Henry Curtis. Naomichi Nakazawa explained the details of the Jikishin Dojo. My wife Charlene assisted me in much of the translation. Mike Sayama also assisted in the translations and editing of the book.

It has been 9 years since I came to Chozen-ji, the temple founded in Hawaii by Omori Roshi to transmit his line of Zen to the West. During this time, Tanouye Tenshin Rotaishi, Archbishop of Daihonzan Chozen-ji, has guided me and supervised all aspects of this book.

Hosokawa Dogen
Honolulu, Hawaii
Spring, 1996

Introduction

In the contemporary Japanese Zen world, there is one man who stands at the top of the mountain. He had a unique way of teaching Zen. His background as an expert in *Kendo* (the Way of the sword) and *Shodo* (the Way of the brush), as a political activist, scholar, and university president is totally different from other Zen masters. Yet outside Japan few would recognize the name of Omori Sogen. Though he has written a great number of books and articles, many have been lost and only a few excerpts from them have been translated into English by Trevor Leggett. I believe that if the story of his life and a part of his teachings were published in English, it would greatly help those who train in Zen in the West.

Although I have known Omori Roshi for over 20 years and re-read much of his writings in preparation for writing this book, I must acknowledge that there are many people in Japan who may be better suited to write this book. I undertook this task only to introduce Omori Roshi to the West with the hope that this book will be like sweet water to one who is thirsty.

I met Omori Sogen Roshi in 1973 during the Rohatsu Dai Sesshin when I was the head monk of Tenryu-ji. Hirata Seiko Roshi, then the Abbot and now the Archbishop, summoned me to receive a donation from a Zen priest. Hirata Roshi told me to thank the man for the donation. Without thinking, I said, "Thank you very much. I know that I am being rude, but may I ask your name?"

He immediately replied, "Omori from Tokyo."

By then I had met many Zen priests so I was very familiar with the kind of energy and presence that they possessed. Omori Roshi, however, was different from all others. I was struck by the strength and blackness of his eyes. The energy emanating from his small five feet two inch frame did not belong to the world of priests. It was so powerful that I could not go close to him. I accepted the donation, and as is the Japanese custom, I accompanied him to the monastery gate. The monastery gate was more than 12 feet tall, yet it seemed very small as Omori Roshi passed through it. He seemed to fill the space like a mountain gliding slowly and regally on a cloud.

A year and a half later in the early autumn of 1975, I entered Seitai-ji International Zen Monastery where Omori Roshi was then the Abbot. I trained there with him for a year and a half. For the next 6 years, despite getting married and succeeding my father as the resident priest of Zuiko-ji in a rural part of Japan, I continued my *koan* training with Omori Roshi. In 1983 he decided my *koan* training was finished and bestowed upon me *inka shomei* (*Dharma* mind-stamp) and told me, "Please carry on after me."

Without hesitation, I replied, "Yes." These words are deeply inscribed in my heart and weigh heavily on my shoulders. As I walk this path, there are even times when I wish I could rid myself of this heavy commitment. The only reason I have been able to make it this far is because I was deeply moved by Omori Roshi. When I said to him, "My goal in life is to become like you," he instantly replied, "You must surpass a person like me."

There is a saying in Buddhism, "The *Dharma* becomes alive and priceless only through the lives of people who practice it." The 1,700 *koan* and the 5,040 *sutra* are dead words until they are embodied in the life of an enlightened person. The story of Omori Roshi's life, which comprises the first part of the book, illustrates how an ordinary human being, not so different from each of us, became the greatest Japanese Zen master of modern time through arduous training. As much as possible, I have used Omori Roshi's own words to tell his story. His text is indented while my comments appear in a regular format.

The second part of the book, The Three Ways, presents the three traditions Omori Roshi trained in. "Way" is a translation of the Japanese *Do* which in turn is a translation of the Chinese *Tao*. A distinctive achievement of Japanese culture was to transform fighting skills such as swordsmanship, fine arts such as calligraphy, and even routine activities such as serving tea into formal disciplines which ultimately lead to the realization of *Tao*. By integrating the Ways of martial arts, Zen, and calligraphy, Omori Roshi developed a unique method of training which has the vitality of the martial arts, the spiritual depth of Zen, and the refinement of the fine arts.

Chapter Four, Zen and *Budo* (Martial Way), is an edited version of the more formal translation by Tanouye Tenshin, Archbishop of Daihonzan Chozen-ji. In this essay Omori Roshi reconciles the seeming contradiction between the martial ways as a method of killing people and Zen as a means of removing delusions and becoming enlightened.

Chapter Five (Practical Zen) and Chapter Six (*Teisho*: The World of the Absolute Present) present Omori Roshi's insights into both the practice and metaphysics of Zen. Practical Zen provides solutions to problems encountered in Zen training. These solutions are based on Omori Roshi's own training and his translation of Buddhist philosophy into practical application. The World of the Absolute Present contains excerpts from Omori Roshi's *teisho* on Sanboin (The Three Truths of the *Dharma*). These excerpts are metaphysical and develop the concept that all Buddhist theory emerges and returns to one principle: *Nirvana* is the point at which time and space intersect. To clearly understand the "I" which exists at this intersection has been the ultimate goal of Zen training since ancient times. When this understanding penetrates one's entire being, it is called *Nirvana* and Freedom. When this "totally free person" acts, Zen art is expressed.

Chapter Seven presents Zen art through Omori Roshi's calligraphy. From the Zen viewpoint, the mere movement of an arm or leg of the "totally free person" is Zen art. Omori Roshi's calligraphy is simply another, perhaps more traditional, window into the art of a Zen master. In any art whether it be a martial art like swordsmanship or a fine art like calligraphy, creativity only emerges from the mastery of technique, but in Zen art creativity must be grounded in the realization of the True Self.

In creative activity, an artist who has mastered technique uses space, time, and energy in a manner which is beyond conscious contrivance. Within his artistic medium he freely expresses his intuitions and insight. For the Zen master, because his creativity is grounded in the realization of the True Self, life itself is the medium of his art. Everything he does, from routine activities to moral decisions, shines with a wondrous quality. Omori Roshi's life was devoted first to the realization of the True Self and then to its expression and endless refinement in swordsmanship, calligraphy, scholarship, politics, and religion. His life is worthy to be considered a masterpiece of Zen art.

PART I

The Life of Omori Sogen

CHAPTER 1

Shugyo

Shugyo: the deepest level of training in the Way.

1904–1934

Childhood

Omori Sogen was born Omori Arinobu in Yamanashi prefecture on March 10, 1904, in a family which descended from the *samurai* class. He received the name Sogen when he became a priest in 1942. He was the fourth child in a family of five children. As a child Omori Roshi was small and quiet until he discovered his strength in the fifth grade. He writes this of his childhood.

> When I was little, I did well in school and was on the quiet side, but in about the fifth grade, I did *Sumo* (Japanese wrestling) with the strongest boy at school. I threw him to the ground with no difficulty. From that time, I developed great confidence in my physical strength and became more and more unruly. In the end, I was taking it upon myself to fight on my older brother's behalf. No matter how strong an opponent appeared, I didn't want to lose.[1]
>
> One day when I went home crying, my father scolded me severely, "Don't you ever come home crying after a fight! Go and hit your opponent with this!" and handed me a *bokuto* (wooden sword). I did what he said and went home.
>
> He then yelled at me, "You idiot! How could you hit your own brother!" It seems that my older brother had gone home crying before I got home and told my father that I had hit him with the sword.
>
> My father had given me the *bokuto* and told me to hit my opponent, but when I did so, my father reproached me sternly. I thought that was ridiculous.[2]

Omori Roshi was told by his mother that he was "too theoretical," so when he was 14 or 15 this theoretical youth began to practice *Kendo* simply to become stronger. At that time he lived in Tokyo and went to Kinjo Intermediate School. His first teacher was Imoto Saburo Yoshiaki of the Hokushin Itto Style. Several years later, Imoto Sensei died, and

Omori Roshi diligently commuted to the Yushinkan of Nakayama Hakudo.

At the age of 19, Omori Roshi became seriously ill. He recalls this below:

> I caught a cold suddenly in January and had a high fever. I was unconscious for most of February and March. I didn't know who I was. At the beginning of March, all of a sudden, I regained consciousness and realized that I was lying on a *futon* (Japanese mattress) on the floor. I had become skin and bones. Then, for the first time since my illness, I ate rice gruel. March 10 was my birthday, so I tried to stand. I did so with great difficulty by holding on to a pillar. My mother said happily, "You stood, didn't you? You stood, didn't you?"
>
> From that time, however, my mother lay sick next to me. Early one morning, she vomited blood and died. When we called the doctor, he said that she had been ill with ulcers before and that her ruptured stomach caused her to vomit blood and die. But the neighborhood women came and told me this, "Ever since you became ill during the coldest part of winter, your mother went to the well every morning without fail and threw cold well water on herself saying, 'Please exchange my life for my child's.' Because you recovered, your mother's life was taken away and she died."
>
> Maybe it was just something said by ignorant women, but I firmly believe what they told me. They were telling the truth. Why did I believe their story? Because, from that time on, I forgot what my mother looked like. Now or even right after her death, though I look at my mother's picture, I can't think that she is my mother. I wonder who this person is. I don't remember my mother's face at all. Because the life that I am now living is my mother's, I cannot look at her as a son would look at his mother. My mother is here; she has become me; I have come to believe this. Because my life is my mother's life, I must take care of it, value my life, and live for as long as I can. I must carry on the life of my mother who died so quickly and so young.[3]

Maeno Sensei and Oda Sensei

Though he had the misfortune to lose his mother, Omori Roshi felt very fortunate because he was able to find excellent teachers. Around the time of his mother's death, he met Maeno Jisui (1870–1940), his first teacher in Zen.

> I met Maeno Sensei during the spring of my nineteenth year. I was a student at Nihon University and also worked part-time. During winter vacation, I sorted New Year's cards at the post office. Once when I had to stay overnight there, I was bored and found the magazine, "Zen and Taoism," published by Maeno Sensei. Because a part of me had been interested in Zen since childhood, I went to see Maeno Sensei right away. He headed an association called Taigendo Shoja. For three years, rain or shine, I went there every night. This was the place where I received my first instruction in the Way.
>
> Maeno Sensei was born in Tosa (in Shikoku). When he was fourteen, he was troubled and frustrated because he couldn't understand *"Chigyo Go Itsu"* ("What you know and what you do are the same," or "the unity of knowing and doing"). Someone told him to see a Zen priest so he went to see Shiragi Jitsuzen Zenji. Jitsuzen Zenji belonged to the Suio Line (following the *dharma* lineage of Hakuin).
>
> While Maeno Sensei was studying at Waseda Law School, now Waseda University, he met Nakahara Toju (Nantenbo). When Nantenbo wanted to give him *inka shomei* ("mind-stamp," certifying his enlightenment), he refused, saying that he didn't need such a thing and that he would receive it directly from Shakyamuni Buddha. Maeno Sensei graduated from Waseda and became a forest ranger because he said that it was more advantageous to train by himself in the mountains. Eventually he became the student of Miyachi Izuo of the Department of the

Imperial Household. He studied Japanese classical literature and *Taoism*. Maeno Sensei was also an expert in the martial arts. He learned swordsmanship from Kurachi Budayu and became a master of the Mugai Style of *Iaido* (the art of drawing and cutting with the sword). He was also an authority on the Takenouchi Style of *Jujitsu*. Besides speaking on Zen, he lectured on Japanese literature, *Shinto* law, and *Taoist* writings. I also heard some of his lectures on Lao Tze.

Maeno Sensei could drink *sake* in quantity. After *sanzen* (private interview with Zen master), Sensei would go into the kitchen and have his evening drink. After I had been going to Taigendo Shoja for a while, he called from the kitchen, "Is that you Omori? Come in for awhile." He said, "Have a drink," and offered me a *sake* cup. I was nineteen, but since I had never drunk, I drank it down in a gulp.

"You can really drink. Have another cup," he said. Again I gulped it down.

"You like *sake*. Have another." So saying, he made me drink. In the end, he taught me how to drink before he taught me *zazen*.

At these "drinking *zazen* sessions," he told me about many things: the "old days," the period of his training and Zen writings, and the literature about hermits. I will never know how much I learned from these sessions because of the wide scope of topics. Maeno Sensei was a very profound man with substantial ability. He said, "I could easily get three or four doctorates if I wanted to." This was no empty boast. Everyone agreed that it was true. This teacher's influence broadened my horizon tremendously.

When we travelled to Korea together, he was reading Marx's *Das Kapital*. Another time, he was reading the *Bible*. Therefore, I, too, read many of Marx's books including *Das Kapital*. Also I read the whole *Bible*, both the old and the new testaments; this taught me a great deal.[4]

Omori Roshi trained with Maeno Sensei for several years before Maeno Sensei returned to his birth place. Omori Roshi was then taught by Oda Sensei to whom Maeno Sensei had entrusted the *dojo*. Maeno Sensei died in 1940, at the age of seventy-one.

Oda Sensei, whose real name was Katsutaro, was from Hiroshima. As a lay student, he received his *inka* from Katsumine Daitetsu (the Archbishop of Nanzen-ji) and assumed the name Tokusui Koji. He was very different from Maeno Sensei. Maeno Sensei was *yuzumuge* (flexible and adaptable to any situation). On the other hand, Oda Sensei was like an ancient *samurai*, very severe and rigid. He had a great knowledge of *Shinto*, Buddhism and Confucianism and could speak German and several other languages. He was also a *Judo* expert.

The explanation on the *"Doctrine of the Mean"* was Oda Sensei's specialty. He had unique views on this doctrine from the physical experience of Zen and *Judo*. For example, about one's center of being, he said, "The center under the *hara*[5] is the dead center. The living center is not located in one specific place; it is

Oda Sensei on far right, Omori Roshi second to right, and Oda Sensei's son on the far left at a ceremony affirming the brotherhood between Omori Roshi and Oda Sensei's son, 1931.

the balance between you and your opponent. When you are grappling with your opponent in a natural position, the living center is probably below your *hara*. But when you are attacked or you attack, the center can be in your toes or in your finger tips. There are two centers: one is the two dimensional center (in stillness), and the other is the three dimensional center (in movement)." It was well-worth listening to this viewpoint.[6]

Yamada Jirokichi

Besides training under Maeno and Oda Sensei, Omori Roshi continued to commute to Yushinkan to practice *Kendo*. From the time he started training at Yushinkan, Omori Roshi had always intended to live the life of a master of *Kendo*. But when he was about 20, he began to seriously question *Kendo* training that was solely concerned with winning or losing. He wondered, "Is what I am doing enough? Going through life fighting with others, will I feel satisfied when I am about to die? Will I feel that my life was worthwhile?" So questioning, Omori Roshi thought of abandoning *Kendo* but found new inspiration in Yamada Jirokichi.

Yamada Sensei's *Kendo* was not the *Kendo* that most of us know which involves striking the *men* (head), *kote* (wrist), and *do* (body) to score points. It was a Way, and according to Omori Roshi "by understanding this Way, one can learn the Great Way of the Universe, and one's character can become complete." Omori Roshi tells of his training with Yamada Sensei below.

> Quite by chance I came across an article in a copy of the magazine *Chuo Ko-ron* entitled, "An Evening Talk on *Kendo*," by Yamada Jirokichi, which said "*Kendo* is not just hitting and thrusting. By understanding this Way, man can learn the Great Way of the universe; one's character can become complete." By

contacting the magazine publisher, I found out where Yamada Sensei lived and went to see him.

That was in 1924. Yamada Sensei was living in a small house. When I met him, I said, "I was very impressed by your article in the magazine. May I become your student?" But he said, "Look, I have no *dojo* at my home. I can't teach you without a *dojo*," and he dismissed me. From that day on, I visited him everyday for one week. One week became ten days. Finally he said, "You are a very persistent fellow. Well, then, come to the *dojo* at Hitotsubashi University." That is how I became a student of Yamada Sensei and began to learn real *Kendo*.

Though Yamada Sensei was the fifteenth generation master of the Jikishin Kage School and was carrying on the Sakakibara *Dojo*, this *dojo* burned down in the Great Kanto Earthquake (September, 1923), so his only *dojo* was at the university. Yamada Sensei was also an intellectual who has left behind many of his own writings. The primary ones are *The Principles of Kendo Schools—Volumes I and II*, *History of Japanese Kendō*, *Kashima Shinden Jikishin Kage Ryu*, and *The Doctrines of Ancient Health Practices*.

Yamada Sensei's *Kendo* was entirely different from what I had studied before. For about half a year all I did was practice how to walk straight while breathing deeply. "Aaaaah (inhaling), Ummmmmm (exhaling), Aaaaah, Ummmmmm." Usually, when my right foot went forward, my belly button moved to the left. It should have been facing forward. Next when my left foot went forward, my belly button faced right. I had to move my *koshi* (lower back and hips) so that my belly button would face straight forward. This is called *shinpo* (correct walking) and was a very basic practice in keeping the body straight. At that time, I already had a black belt ranking, but I was not permitted to hold either a bamboo sword or a wooden sword.

The chronicles of the Jikishin Kage School state this as the essence of the school: *Korai shutai no yokei o nozoki, honrai seimei no gotai ni fuku suru ni ari* (Cut all habits you have acquired since the day you were born and return to your Original Nature). With this in mind, I have practiced *Kendo* until now.

Very often Yamada Sensei would stand in the entrance of the *dojo* with a bamboo sword in hand. When a student casually entered the *dojo*, he would hit his shin sharply with the bamboo sword and say, "*Kendo* does not start after you enter the *dojo* and put on your equipment. It starts from the morning. No, it started from the time you were born." I didn't understand why *Kendo* began at the time of birth and was often hit!

Later I understood that man is continually in relation with other things. For example, in the morning when we get up, we wash our face. We confront the mirror; we confront water; we confront the toothbrush. When we wash our face with water, we feel that the water is cold and think, "It's so cold. How unpleasant!" The water says, "*men!*" (a successful strike to the head in *Kendo*). It has hit us and taken a point on us.

As a man leaves his house for work, it is raining. If he thinks, "I wish I could have a day off on a day like this," the weather gets a point. In this way, we are in opposition with things and others. All day long we are doing *Kendo*.

That is why if we truly understand the correct way to communicate between person and person, we can complete the Way of humanity. That is what Yamada Sensei taught and how I have developed my view of *Kendo*.[7]

During this time that Omori Roshi was immersed in *Kendo* and *zazen*, he became so skillful that he could kill flies with a sword, and his body was so strong that the man who measured Roshi's chest during his medical examination for conscription in 1924 asked, "Are you a stonecutter?" As a result of his severe training, Roshi, who was only five feet two inches, had a chest that measured 40 inches. During this time Omori Roshi also had a run in with the police.

There are no known photographs of Omori Roshi at age 20 but this picture, taken at age 41, shows how well he maintained his condition.

I guess I was around 20. I was living with a few young men in a rented house in Sugamo (in Tokyo). Near the house was Somei Cemetery. Every evening, I would go for a walk there, and one time, I wondered, "If I push those stone lanterns that are lined up, would they fall down? I'm going to try."

I was training in *Kendo* everyday and was very proud of my brute strength, but still I couldn't move a lantern. It bothered me so much that I went there every night. Eventually, my repeated efforts were rewarded, and I was able to push a lantern over. If I did it correctly, the stone that was on the very top and the bamboo hat shaped rock that was right beneath it would fall, roll, hit each other, and break. When I saw the broken pieces, I got very excited. It became an obsession, and I went out every night to overturn a lantern. In the end, I overturned all the stone lanterns in the cemetery. I was reported to the police and arrested.

When I was taken to the police station, I was wearing my *montsuki* (formal kimono with the family crest). I was told that such clothing was impertinent by the police officer in charge. I said, "Why is this impertinent? This is Japanese formal attire." A policeman suddenly hit me. I hit back with all my might. We got into a fight that became a wrestling match. From another room seven or eight detectives came flying in and tried to hold me down. Since I was so violent, they grabbed my hair, pushed me down, and beat me with a wooden sword. There were a lot of them so I was beaten terribly. At that time, I thought that if only they had not been able to make me fall, I would not have lost. That's why I decided to study *Judo*.

I was in jail for twenty-nine days. There I met Matsuda Hidegoro who had been put in jail for fighting. He was only three years older than me and was a third degree black belt Kodokan *Judo* student. Since I had become interested in *Judo*, he was a good person to talk with.

When I was finally sent to the public prosecutor's office, I was found not guilty. In jail the pickpockets and robbers had told me to tell the prosecutor that I knew nothing about the incident, and that, as a result of being tortured, I had been forced to sign the statement. Before my arrest, I used to do *sumo* with my friends. We threw each other into the walls over and over again so I had wounds all over my body. I showed my scars to the prosecutor and said, "As you see, my body is covered with wounds as the result of being tortured."

When I was freed, I immediately went to Kodokan and began *Judo* training. Matsuda, who had been freed before me, had become a fourth ranked *Judo* student and was very arrogant. In prison he was my junior, however, so when I said, "Matsuda," he replied, "Oh, you came." From then on, we became good friends. For ten years, I practiced both *Judo* and *Kendo*.[8]

Hojo

In his training with Yamada Sensei, Omori Roshi eventually advanced from *shinpo* (walking practice) to the *Hojo*. The *Hojo* is a sword form originated by Matsumoto Bizen no kami Naokatsu in the middle of the Muromachi period (1333–1573). He received the teachings of the *Hojo* in a dream. The *Hojo* consists of four parts, each representing one of the four seasons: *Hasso Happa* (blasting from the position with the sword held above the head) is like the spirit of the rising sun which breaks forth in spring; *Itto Ryodan* (one sword split in two) is like the blazing summer sun that scorches; *Uden Saden* (right turn/left turn, changes, transformation) is like autumn leaves falling from a tree; *Chotan Itchi Mi* (long/short in oneness) is like the *ki* (energy) of the grass and trees that returns to their roots in winter. Ten minutes of intense concentration are required to perform the exacting movements of the *Hojo*.

In 1929 Omori Roshi underwent the grueling practice of doing the *Hojo* a hundred times a day for seven days. He recounts his experience below.

> Onishi Hidetaka, who was captain of the *Kendo* Club of Hitotsubashi University, and I were told by Yamada Sensei, "In our style, after completing the *hyappon keiko* (one hundred time practice) one is able to receive the final certificate." It was decided that at the end of July, we would be confined to a mountain temple in Yamanashi prefecture. After 20 days of preparation we began the *hyappon keiko*.
>
> We got up at 4:00 in the morning, went down the mountain, and bathed in a river. Before breakfast we did the *Hojo* 15 times. After that we rested awhile then practiced 30 more times. After lunch we rested and did the *Hojo* 55 more times until dusk. We did *zazen* in the evenings.
>
> By the third day I could shout more loudly and powerfully during practice, but my voice was so hoarse I could not speak at all. At night my body was so hot that I couldn't sleep. Food would not go down my throat; I had only water and raw eggs. My urine was the color of blood. The arms that held the wooden sword could not be raised. We were resigned to death. I couldn't go before Yamada Sensei and say, "I failed." Onishi and I got out our notes and letters and burned them all as we prepared to die.
>
> On the fourth day, a strange thing happened. The same arms that had difficulty in even holding the wooden sword went up

smoothly over my head. As my arms went down, I felt a strength that was not physical coming out of both arms. It felt as if this downward cut extended to the other end of the world.

For seven days, we practiced the *Hojo* a hundred times daily in this manner. We finally finished at the beginning of September. Later Yamada Sensei praised me saying, "That is the Muso (No-thought) Style." I was able to cultivate mental strength entirely because of this *Hojo*.[9]

Toyama Mitsuru and Toyama Ryusuke

Toyama Mitsuru (1855–1944) emerged from a background of poverty and *samurai* idealism in the streets of Fukuoka to create a new patriotic, social order which linked political rightists and the underworld of the *yakuza* (Japanese organized crime). He founded the Dark Ocean and Black Dragon Societies and had deep ties in the government of Japan in the 1920's and 30's. He and his son Toyama Ryusuke profoundly influenced Omori Roshi's character. Omori Roshi recalls his association with them below.

Toyama Mitsuru lost his Akasaka home in the major Kanto earthquake (1923) and lived in his son Ryusuke's home for awhile. Nearby lived Mr. Shindo, a close friend. One day when I went to visit Mr. Shindo, the two of them were playing *go* (Japanese chess). For a while I watched them from the corridor. After the game ended as Mr. Toyama left, I went around to the entrance of the house to say good-bye. He looked toward me and nodded. One hand held a cane, and one hand was on his chest. Although he was well into his sixties, he looked like a golden haired lion majestically leaving his lair. I felt a great degree of power and authority emanate from him.

Mr. Shindo said, "Mr. Toyama underwent a complete change after he became 50. Before 50, he was the kind of man who could step on a man's head with his tall *geta* (Japanese wooden slippers) and think nothing of it. But after fifty, he became a changed man. People's happiness became his happiness; people's sadness became his sadness." Once when Mr. Toyama was on a walk, a dog bit him. He took the dog to his kitchen and said, "This dog bit me. He looks very hungry. Give him something to eat."

Another time, someone told Mr. Toyama of another person's faults. Mr. Toyama responded, "Among ten things that man must have at least one good point. Associate with that one good point." He didn't bother with the bad points but worked with the good points. He could see the good in a person. I tried to do the same thing but the bad points of people seemed to stick out. It was most depressing.

In another incident, Yokoyama Sensei (Omori Roshi's calligraphy teacher) saw a scroll by Saigo Takamori (the general who led the forces of the Meiji Restoration) hanging on the second floor of

Toyama Mitsuru, seated in the front row center, at a gathering of regional right-wing leaders (c. 1935).

the Toyama home. He told me, "Omori, that is a fake. For a man like Mr. Toyama to have an imitation hanging in his home is a disgrace. You go and tell him." Because he told me this, I asked Mr. Toyama, "Is this Saigo calligraphy authentic?"

He answered calmly, "Yes, it is from the time when he was studying the O-ie style."

I asked, "Did Saigo practice the O-ie style?"

"Ho, ho, ho," he laughed in his unique way.

I thought, "Darn it!" and asked again, "Don't you think that this is an imitation?"

He told me, "I am not hanging a scroll by Saigo Takamori. This was given to me by Sugiyama. I am hanging Sugiyama's *kokoro* (heart, mind, feelings)."

Since Yokoyama Sensei told me to tell Mr. Toyama about the scroll, I did. But I made a fool of myself! In consideration for the giver, Mr. Toyama had hung the scroll; he didn't care if it was an imitation or not.[10]

As much as Omori Roshi admired Toyama Mitsuru, his son Ryusuke inspired him even more deeply. Omori Roshi always repeated, "I feel very thankful to have been able to meet this kind of man (Ryusuke) during my lifetime."

> My calligraphy teacher, Yokoyama Sensei had a very sharp eye for art. In evaluating Ryusuke Sensei's calligraphy, he said, "Because of his age, Mr. Toyama has more depth and Ryusuke Sensei is still behind his father. But in greatness of character he will probably surpass his father. Judging from his calligraphy, he is, by nature, a great man, one man out of several hundred."

All the people that I have spoken about so far may not have been famous, but each was on the highest level in his field. I don't think that Toyama Ryusuke was a specialist in any field, but even if you put all of the other men together, they could not come close to the greatness of this man. I met him in the summer of 1925. One day Mr. Shindo asked me, "How about going to meet Toyama Ryusuke?" I had previously heard that Toyama Mitsuru's eldest son was an idiot, but that he was very good in *go*. I went to see him. Toyama Ryusuke had a lung disease and had to rest quietly, but when I went to see him, he was wearing a *kimono* (Japanese robe), sitting very erect. He was alone; he had a book on *go* in one hand and was calmly moving the *go* pieces.

He didn't look like a person who was ill. His figure was thin but he was like a mountain. Here was no idiot but a truly great man of the type one can only meet once in a lifetime.

When he entered Dobun Shoin College, Ryusuke was very quiet and didn't stand out. It so happened, however, that Sasaki Moko-o, a well-known politician gave a speech at Dobun Shoin. People say that there was some kind of falsehood in his speech. Ryusuke Sensei silently stood up, and began to walk calmly toward the platform. He took hold of Moko-o's wrist and pulled him down from the platform. Everyone sat stupefied. Even Moko-o could not utter a single word. Ryusuke Sensei must have had considerable inner force.

During his university days, Ryusuke would go to lectures in very formal clothing wearing a *haori* (formal Japanese jacket with the family crest) and *hakama* (formal Japanese skirt worn by men and women). He would nod at every word the professor uttered saying, "Umm, Umm," while taking notes with a brush in characters that were one square inch large. Before a test his friends would teach him for two or three hours, feeling that if they had taught him that much it should be all right. When they asked, "Well, did you understand?" He would reply, "I don't understand at all." Everyone was so amazed and disgusted that they were speechless. It is said that even his mother criticized him, saying, "He is like a long spring day added to a long autumn night." He was indeed a very slow moving person, but he was also very patient. He was a warm and quiet man of few words. But when angered, he had tremendous force like a fierce lion. One of his roars would make most people cower.

He rarely got angry, but I experienced his anger once during the time of the Manchurian Incident. My *sempai* (senior), was with the *Asahi Newspaper* and was a friend of the prime minister of that time, Konoe Fumimaro. I was asked by my *sempai* to see if Ryusuke's father would go to Chung-king as Konoe's representative. I took this request too lightly and accepted it. When I asked him, Mr. Toyama would not give me an answer, so I spoke to Ryusuke to speak to his father. Since it was such an important matter, I thought that he would agree.

He did not answer, however, and was silent. To my surprise I noticed that Ryusuke's eyes began to fill with tears. Suddenly, he opened his eyes and said, "Are you telling my father to die? If you are telling him to die, all right. I, myself, will tell my father, 'Go to China and die.'" His eyes were closed for awhile. Then he opened his eyes, still full of tears, and thundered, "Can a cat use a tiger! What has Japan come to?" (At this time Toyama Mitsuru had more power in Japan than Prime Minister Konoe.)

I had just entered my thirties and was twenty years younger than Ryusuke but I began to tremble because of the force of these words. I asked Ryusuke Sensei to please let this matter pass and to pretend as if the question had never been raised.

Ryusuke Sensei's compassion was also awe inspiring. A very good friend who was staying in the same college dormitory had tuberculosis. Seeing this depressed and despairing person vomit blood, Ryusuke Sensei said, "Tuberculosis is nothing. Watch this!" and drank down the vomited blood.

If you say it is absurd, it is absurd. If you say that he had no knowledge of hygiene, he had none. But it is in such actions where he was unique. He was not able to console his sick friend through words. It is said that as part of his training in *jyo-e funi* (clean and unclean are one and the same), Yamaoka Tesshu swallowed the vomit of a drunk beggar. But, for Ryusuke Sensei, this was not training. It was an awkward but very warm way to console his friend. For him, it was all he could do.

It is not clear whether he became infected because he swallowed the vomit or because he was living with this friend. When his friend passed away, he carried the ashes to the friend's parents in Kagoshima. Upon his return, he caught a cold and had fever. From then on, he was bedridden with an incurable disease.

Toyama Ryusuke in formal attire during the period when he was generally bedridden with tuberculosis (1940).

Perhaps because he had been spoiled, Ryusuke's younger brother had become a problem. To help this brother, their father had arranged to go to their cottage in Gotenba to lecture on the Analects of Confucius somewhere nearby. One day hearing of this, Ryusuke suddenly sat up on his sick bed, and said, "My father is having a difficult time because of my younger brother. I can't be still and just lie here. I will go to Gotenba immediately." Ryusuke was the oldest son, and since his father was trying his best to help his brother, it would not do for him to go by car or train. This bedridden person got up and said that he would walk from Kugenuma to Gotenba (some 40 miles away). On the way there was a sudden rain shower, and he spent the night in the shelter of a shrine. He caught a cold, and his condition worsened. That is how sincere he was.

For a person who had stayed in bed for several years to say that he is going to walk somewhere shows tremendous strength of spirit. Even though he was bedridden, he could raise the spirits of those around him. He could do this because of the strength of his will power.

Because a man like Ryusuke existed in this world, there is still hope. Because he lived, I too can become that kind of man. That is the feeling he gave. But when I think of my own self, my roots are inferior so I cannot become selfless like Ryusuke, I cannot completely discard my ego. Nonetheless, even if it is only by one step, then my wish is to get closer to the attainment of that state of Ryusuke's.

Ryusuke Sensei often read the Diamond *Sutra*. He said that since he would be reading it, he may as well learn to recite it without the scripture book. For one week, he went without sleep and learned the entire *sutra*. With a candle on both elbows, he continuously read the *sutra* with his hands in *gassho*. Though even an expert finds it difficult to memorize that long *sutra*, he memorized it in a week. This proves that not only did he possess strong will, but also an extraordinary brain.

Someone recounted to me another story which shows Ryusuke's tremendous willpower:

There was to be a commemoration of the tenth anniversary of the death of Sun Yat-sen (the revolutionary leader who overthrew imperial rule in China). From Japan, Ryusuke's father Mitsuru, Premier Inukai, and others were to attend. Despite the illness that he had suffered for eight or nine years, Ryusuke Sensei resolved to leave his bed and go to China. In the intense heat of June this very long Chinese ceremony was held. Some people held their hats to shield themselves from the sun; some people opened their fans; even healthy people could not stay still. During it all, Ryusuke maintained a resolute demeanor and did not move at all from beginning till end. That sick man did that, you know. When I saw his figure, I came to realize the greatness of this man and to revere him.

As I said before, Ryusuke Sensei was bedridden for a long time. When he heard a person's story, he often just put his hands together in *gassho* and smiled gently, but he had a strange gift: if one spent an hour with him, one would be full of energy for one week. We all had difficult times and problems and felt frustrated. At those times, we would go to see this sick man. Since he was a man of very few words, there were times when we went to see him and left without him saying a word. When we went home, however, the feeling of frustration was gone, and one would be full of energy. Moreover, that feeling would continue for a week and sometimes more.

Instead of comforting a sick man, we were comforted by the sick man. At the beginning, I thought that he had that effect on only me, but all who went to see him went home saying, "Today I was comforted by Ryusuke."

In Buddhism, there is a word, *semui,* which means to give fearlessness. Ryusuke Sensei was an example of a true *semuisha* (giver of fearlessness).

One day when I went to see him, Ryusuke Sensei's cheek was swollen. I asked him what had happened and he said, "About a week ago, the dentist came and pulled out my tooth. But he had a difficult time, and I began to bleed profusely. The dentist was distraught and in a greasy sweat. Holding a washbowl, he began going back and forth. 'Doctor! I am the one who is bleeding—not you!' I said. He said, 'Oh, yes,' and calmed down a bit." Relating this story, Ryusuke Sensei laughed.

A few days later, I learned that Ryusuke Sensei was in serious condition and rushed to see him. His father was at his side holding his hand. He was unconscious and moaning. When his tooth was pulled, a virus entered his body, and he got blood poisoning. It went to his brain, became meningitis, and he died.

When Ryusuke Sensei died, his father was at his side stroking his head. He spoke to Ryusuke as though he were alive. He said, "Ryusuke, you had a splendid life. Most people in your condition would have died twenty years ago, but you hung on until now. If one lives for a hundred years but never grasps the essence of life, that life was not worthwhile. But you certainly knew what was important in life. Very well done."[11]

Seki Seisetsu

During the late spring of 1925, when he was twenty-one, Omori Roshi met Seki Seisetsu (1877–1945) who became his lifetime mentor and his greatest teacher. Seisetsu was born on January 18, 1877, in Hyogo Prefecture with the family name of Kabumoto. At the age of two he was adopted by Seki Soshun of Tenrin-ji, a temple under the jurisdiction of Tenryu-ji. At age five, he became a *kozo* (child apprentice monk). In February of 1893, at the age of 16, he entered Tenryu-ji Monastery and began *sanzen* under Hashimoto Gasan.

After the death of Gasan, he continued *sanzen* under Touiku. In 1902 at the age of 25, Seisetsu returned to Tenrin-ji but resigned a year later and did *sanzen* with Takagi Ryoen at Tokkoin in Kobe. At the age of 30, he received *inka shomei* (certifying his realization) from Takagi Ryoen. In 1922 he became the abbot of Tenryu-ji, and in 1943, at the age of 66, became the head of all the Rinzai temples in Japan. He died at the age of 68 on October 2, 1945.

Below Omori Roshi recollects his meeting and training with Seisetsu.

> I was taking a walk on Kagurazaka (in Tokyo) when I saw a sign saying, "The Archbishop of Tenryu-ji, Seki Seisetsu *Zazen Kai.*" I went in and listened to Seisetsu Roshi's discourse. Right away, I went to tell Oda Sensei what I had heard. He said, "All right, I will check this man out."
>
> When he returned, he urged me, "That priest Seki Seisetsu is very intelligient. If you have a teacher who lacks in intelligence, you

will suffer. You must by all means practice *sanzen* with that priest." I immediately went to Meitokukai, the place where Seisetsu Roshi was lecturing, and became a student of Seki Seisetsu.

Seisetsu Roshi was about 50 at this time. He was sitting on a chair on the second floor of the Meitokukai. He impressed me as a huge *oyabun* (chief) with piercing eyes who spoke very sparingly. It was difficult to get close to him.

I started *sanzen* in the traditional manner with *mu* (the first *koan* usually given to beginners). In the beginning, I went once a year from Tokyo to Tenryu-ji in Kyoto for the *rohatsu sesshin* (the one week *sesshin* commemorating Buddha's enlightenment). In addition, I went every month to Meitokukai in Tokyo for *sanzen*.

Once I overheard Seisetsu Roshi tell a student in another room, "In May, the weather is nice, so come."

Very cautiously and timidly I asked, "May I come to the *sesshin* in May, too?"

"Yes, come. Come." he said.

I thought, "That means I can go anytime." I went to the May *sesshin*. In one year, I went to two big *sesshin*; in the end, I went to all *sesshin* every year.

Seisetsu Roshi was a severe man but there was another aspect to him. Once after *sesshin*, when I went to tell Seisetsu Roshi

Seki Seisetsu in his late 60's.

that I would be returning to Tokyo, he said, "Good. I have to go to Kyoto Station to see the mayor off. Sorry to bother you, but if you don't mind, would you carry his present and come with me to the station?"

When we went to Kyoto Station, Seisetsu Roshi said, "There is still time till the train departs. Let's go to see the art exhibition at the department store." I followed him into the store and we went to the exhibition. He looked around at the exhibition saying, "Hmm. Hmm." After making one round, we left and went up to the roof.

Looking to the east, he said, "That is Mt. Hiei." He faced north and said, "Kurama is around there." He moved around on the roof slowly muttering so that I could hear. At first, while following him, I wondered what he was doing, but finally I understood. Since Seisetsu Roshi knew that I always went to Kyoto just for *sesshin* and returned to Tokyo as soon as it was over, he made up an excuse and was showing Kyoto to me from the roof of this department store. For that reason, he made me carry the present for the mayor and brought me here. When I realized what he was doing, I was touched beyond words.

When I began going to *sesshin* at Tenryu-ji, particularly during the December *rohatsu sesshin*, I would think, this time, I will die the "Great Death" (*Tai-Shi Ichi-Ban*). But by the evening of the first day, I would be already tired. Going out to do *yaza* (*zazen* done by oneself), it was cold. I thought, "If I feel so tired today, I will be no good tomorrow so I will end for today." I would return to my place and go to sleep.

The next day, I would think, "This is no good," and try hard. During the afternoon, however, I would become tired. My legs hurt. I had stiff shoulders. By the time I went out to do *yaza*, I was sleepy and again would think, "If I overdo it tonight, all I will do tomorrow is doze during *zazen*, and it will not be good." Thinking these things, I would go back to my place and sleep. Though I was doing *zazen* in order to destroy my ego, I pampered myself and could not do it. I think that this was a pitiful attitude.

After risking my life during the Hundred-times Practice of the *Hojo*, I guess I gained confidence. With that confidence, I thought that even if I died, I would not regret it. This time at *sesshin*, even if it was midnight, even if it was dawn, I didn't feel that I should go to sleep because I might be tired the next day. I sat intently. *Zazen* is just one stroke of the valorous mind

The Entrance Hall (Genkan) at Tenryu-ji, Kyoto.

(*yumiyo*). Without this valorous mind, this feeling of casting aside the myriad distractions, one cannot do *zazen*.

During a summer *sesshin* while we were lined up sitting in front of the *kansho* (the bell which is rung before going in for *sanzen*), the hair on the nape of the monk in front of me was trembling. "Could he be that tense about *sanzen*?" I wondered. We laymen rang the *kansho* bell with a nonchalant feeling as if we were playing, but the "professional" monk was deadly serious. When I saw that, I was amazed and surprised. Was I doing only lukewarm *sanzen*? This young monk who must have been younger than me was so tense that the hair on his head, which had only been shaved four or five days ago, was shaking. I can still clearly see it. I shuddered at the sight. My skin crawled. I thought that it was a frightful thing and wondered if being a professional priest was so forbidding.

As for my *koan*, one, two, three years went by but Roshi would not approve. It wasn't that he wouldn't permit me to go on. He would say to me, "I could let you pass, but what about you, is it all right with you?" What could I say? Another time, he said "If you were a monk who was here just to put in time to become the head priest of a temple, I would be much more lenient. If not, monks would have to pass their whole life without opening their eye, and it would be shameful for them. That would be too pitiful. Therefore, I let them pass more easily. Also if they are priests, they will have many opportunities to train. But you are a layman. You began to train of your own volition. As a layman, you don't know if you will be able to train for your whole life. So, when you train, you must be serious and stake your life on your training. I can't let you pass at an intermediate level." He continued, "Even someone like me was so very, very happy when I passed my first *koan* that I danced around Sogenchi (the lake at Tenryu-ji) all night. Do you have that kind of feeling?"[12]

The Zendo at Tenryu-ji serves as both meditation hall and living quarters for the unsui *(trainees).*

For eight years, Omori Roshi commuted between Kyoto and Tokyo. In 1933, finally, he "broke through" and passed the *koan Mu*. About this realization, Omori Roshi says:

> My experience was not very impressive or glorious, so I don't like to talk about it but.... One day after finishing *zazen*, I went to the toilet. I heard the sound of the urine hitting the back of the urinal. It made a splashing sound. It sounded very loud to me, and at the very moment I realized, "AHA," and I understood. I had a realization.
>
> "I AM!" I was very happy. But it was not a showy experience. It was not even very clean. Sound is not the only thing which can trigger this experience. Yamada Mumon Roshi, with whom I trained, had a very different experience. He was walking down the hallway when he saw the red color of the autumn leaves, and suddenly he was enlightened.
>
> When you are enlightened, you realize very clearly that you are right in the middle of *Mu*. This becomes a little theoretical, but according to Nishida's philosophy, it is stated that the infinite circle has infinite centers. In effect, what happens is that you realize that that center of the infinite circle is you.
>
> When you are in the state of *samadhi*, whether you call it *Mu-samadhi* or another type of *samadhi*, you are unconditionally in the realm of Absolute Nothingness (*zettai-mu*). At that time, because of some incident, when you break through the *samadhi*, you will attain realization. (It is like a ripe fruit on a tree. When the wind blows or the branch sways, the fruit will just fall from the tree. If the fruit is not ripe, though the wind may blow or the branch sway, the fruit will not fall).
>
> You will realize with your entire being that you are at the center of Absolute Nothingness (*zettai-mu*) and at the center of the infinite circle. To be at the center of the infinite circle in this human form is to be BUDDHA himself. You have been saved

from the beginning. You will understand all of these things clearly and with certainty.

Even if you are in the state of *samadhi* but do not have this realization, you are merely in that state. You will not feel that, "I am glad I am who I am. A great burden has been lifted from my shoulders. I am content. I am saved."[13]

Omori also did *sanzen* with Harada Sogaku of Hosshin-ji in Obama, Fukui Prefecture. He recounts his experience below.

> In the *zendo* (meditation hall) of Hosshin-ji, there was a big pillar clock. It helped me to enter *samadhi*. Since this monastery was of the Soto Sect, we meditated with our faces towards the wall, and the *jikijitsu* (head monk of the meditation hall) patrolled behind us. When I went to *sesshin*, the *jikijitsu* and the *jokei* (his assistant) would hold the *keisaku* (a flattened oak stick) and would make their rounds hitting us from the rear.
>
> During the last sitting of a *sesshin*, we would say, "*Muuu*," like the sound a cow makes. They would say that the way the word was voiced was not good and would hit us on the back with all their might. They really hit at that monastery. In the morning as soon as we would get up, wash our faces, and sit on the straw mats, they began to hit us. They would say, "What is this?! You jellyfish!" The way that they hit was terrible. For some reason, however, I was never hit.
>
> When I was sitting one evening, I was saying, "*mu*" and sitting in *zazen* meditation. The head monk came up from behind me and said, "That's good. Keep it up. Without a doubt, you will have a realization." He passed without hitting me. After lights out, everyone would choose a place to do free meditation. No matter where I went, I heard, "*Mu, Mu.*" It was like being in a cow shed. Here in one week, I was told that I had had a realization, but I was not satisfied and went to Seisetsu Roshi to do *sanzen*.

In trying to find an answer to a *koan*, if you say, "*Mu, Mu,*" in a very tired way with the words coming out in a mechanical fashion, no matter how long you practice that, you will never enter *samadhi*. Instead, you must become very serious and say, "*Mu... Mu,*" with your entire body and whole being as you breathe each breath. If you yourself do not BECOME *Mu*, it will not be the correct interpretation of the *koan*.[14]

Atsumi Masaru

While doing *sanzen* with Seisetsu Roshi, Omori Roshi was profoundly influenced by another man. In 1927 he met Atsumi Masaru, who was neither a martial artist nor a Zen master, but a philosopher and a social crusader. Omori Roshi reminisces below.

> Atsumi Sensei was from Hikone in Shiga prefecture. From high school, he went to Kyoto University to study German law, but he didn't study law at all. He persistently looked for and read books on philosophy and Western history. In the end, though he was at the university for four years, he did not graduate.
>
> He was interested in life and society's problems. He read extensively on Christianity, *Shinshu*, and Zen, but he found no inner peace and continued to meditate seriously. He said that quite unexpectedly all of his doubts were resolved with the one word *mikoto* from the *Kojiki*, (Japan's oldest book recording events from the mythical past), and he became a new man. According to Atsumi Sensei, *mikoto* means to know how to use one's life. I was deeply influenced by Atsumi Sensei's "*seimei soku shimei*" ("the way to use one's life").
>
> When I met Atsumi Sensei, his philosophy was to combine the cultures of East and West and to create a new culture which

was unrelated to narrow-minded nationalism. During 1928, the last year of his life, Atsumi Sensei travelled for fifty days from spring to summer on a lecture tour. I was with him the whole time. This was for me my "virgin voyage" on the lecture circuit. I was twenty-four. I was jeered terribly and had to give my lecture during the intervals between the jeering. I didn't leave until I said all that I had to say. Atsumi Sensei then said to me with enthusiasm, "You did very well. If you had tried to leave the platform before you said all that you were supposed to, I was prepared to knock you down with all my might."

One time in Osaka I made all the preparations for the lecture, but I encountered a very big problem. When I went to the police station to discuss the lecture, they told me to bring the document of consent from the lecture hall. When I went to the lecture hall, they told me that I needed the approval of the police. There was nothing I could do so I returned to our lodging.

We were staying with one of Astumi Sensei's students who was a public prosecutor. Atsumi Sensei was leisurely playing *go* with his student. When he saw me, he asked, "You returned before completing your work, didn't you?" Then he yelled, "How could you return before finishing your task? It's like showing your back to the enemy!" This was the Atsumi style of training.

Pretending, I said, "I just returned for a short break," and set out again. I was at wit's end, but I could not retreat. I mustered my courage, gave up any thought of failure, and went back to the lecture hall. I said, "The police have given their consent. The official papers will be delivered later," and borrowed the lecture hall arbitrarily. I paid the fee for the hall, went to the police with the receipt, and finally received official approval. This became a wonderful lesson for me. Atsumi Sensei taught me the spirit of how to cut through any difficulty with resolution.[15]

Yokoyama Setsudo

By travelling and lecturing with Atsumi Sensei throughout Japan, Omori Roshi's field of activity enlarged to encompass not only the martial arts but also politics. Through Atsumi, in 1927 or 1928, Omori Roshi became close to Yokoyama Setsudo, a teacher of Japanese calligraphy. Omori Roshi relates his training with him.

When I first met him, Yokoyama Sensei was in his 40's, about 20 years older than me. He was a librarian at Tokyo University. I wondered what kind of work a librarian did and went to see him. Sensei was sitting on a small stand in the entrance of the library doing *zazen*. The students who passed by were saying, "This old fellow climbed a persimmon tree when he was little and fell. Since then, he has been strange." Listening to their comments, he feigned ignorance and continued to do *zazen*.

When he was about 20, Yokoyama Sensei went to a temple of the Soto sect in Yamagata Prefecture and became the student of the priest there. His priestly name at that time was Setsudo. He then came to Tokyo and had a job lighting the gas street lamps. From around this time he started to let his hair grow. When I met him, his hair was tied in a pony tail with a purple cord; he looked very dashing, like a masterless *samurai*.

When asked why he let his hair grow, he answered, "In the beginning, I did it because I wanted to look different from others, but after it had grown long, I found it convenient. When the weather was hot or cold, I didn't need a hat; the hair protected my head. It's very convenient."

Yokoyama Sensei invited me to his house on Sundays to learn calligraphy, but before beginning to write, he made me do *zazen* for the duration of three sticks of incense (one stick burns for about 45 minutes). I dozed during the first sitting. When I thought the sitting should be ending, I opened my eyes only to see Yokoyama Sensei lighting another incense stick. I thought, "We will sit for the duration of another stick." Though my legs hurt, I sat through the second one. After the second one, Mrs. Yokoyama got up to prepare lunch. I was very envious of her. When I saw Yokoyama Sensei lighting another stick of incense, I got irritated and thought, "What is this old man doing? He should stop already. Why does he have to light three? I'd like to punch him!" I was so irritated. I couldn't sit well during the third stick of incense. Only after that did we begin to draw.

Yokoyama Sensei's school of calligraphy was called Jubokudo. He had been the student of a man called Chodo Ryuzen. Chodo Ryuzen was a priest of the Tendai Sect and was teaching Jubokudo at a place called the Ryuzen Association. Although I was not really a student of the student of Chodo, through Yokoyama Sensei's recommendation I was able to receive my teacher's certificate as Chodo's direct student. If we hadn't done that, people could have said that I was not qualified to teach.

Yokoyama-sensei in his study.

Shugyo (1904–1934)

In the beginning, we didn't write as we do now. We wrote more quickly and lightly. After awhile, many students from the *Kendo* division of Hitotsubashi University began to study with Yokoyama Sensei. Because he was also studying the *Hojo* at the University, gradually the spirit of *Kendo* and calligraphy naturally mixed. Slowly *Hitsuzendo* (the Way of the Brush) took shape.

Every year during his summer vacation, Yokoyama Sensei would shut himself in a cave near Mt. Akagi's Fudo Waterfall for 40 days. I asked Sensei if I could go too, and so, twice I spent time in that cave. I have many memories of those times. Once he said to me, "I am 40 already, but even now, I dream of my English and mathematics tests and groan." That is how poorly he did in English and mathematics. He said that he worked and studied at the same time, finally graduating from school when he was 28.

Another time he said, "All you do is martial arts so you don't know how to relax. You must develop a feeling for the fine arts. I will teach you a pack-horse driver's song!" He made me sing, but only after doing *zazen* in the cave for one or two hours. He said to project my voice from the bottom of my abdomen. Then he made me pronounce the sound, "*O*" from the beginning of the pack-horse driver's song which goes, "*Oshoro takashima.*"

"*Oooooo.*"

"No. No. No good." He made me do this for about a week. "You're no good. You are tone deaf. Let's quit," he said, and I was expelled from the singing lessons.

Later both Yokoyama Sensei and I studied voice from an expert on popular singing called Mishima who had gone to France to study voice correctly. Mishima said, "Yokoyama Sensei is truly tone deaf. His musical scales are mixed up. You are more correct." The more correct one had been expelled. This is the kind of thing that happened on Mt. Akagi.

Because Yokoyama Sensei's character and mine are exact opposites, there were many things that we didn't like about each other, but there were many things that drew us together. To Yokoyama Sensei, who was not a man of quick wit, I seemed a very dangerous and rowdy man of talent. I studied calligraphy with him, and he commented on it in detail. He would say, "An unsheathed sword will wound by itself; put it back into its scabbard. Cultivate virtue; not showing one's talent is superb." He would praise and criticize me. He criticized my intelligence often. Personally I didn't think that I was particulary intelligent. He would also scold me, saying, "You have a tendency to surround the other person on four sides so that he cannot escape. You draw him to you, and then you kill him."

I detested the criticism, "You have talent." It bothered me so much that I consulted a physiognomist. I asked him, "I have been told by someone that I have talent and that I should hide that talent. What should I do?"

That physiognomist was kind enough to say, "Your talent was given to you by the heavens to use in this world. If you don't use it, don't you think that the treasure will rot? I won't say to throw your talent away as Yokoyama Sensei has said. I would like to say that you should use your talent to the fullest."

When I heard that, I was no longer bothered by the words, "You have talent." I became more relaxed. Whether I had talent or not didn't matter. I began to feel that it was all right to be just how I was. If I showed talent in my calligraphy, however, I thought that I had to erase it somehow. It became my lifelong task. Thankfully, the critique I received after I became 50 was, "Your talent has gradually disappeared." It is all thanks to Yokoyama Sensei.

I had trained under Seisetsu Roshi but I never received such criticism. He helped me with my *koan* and led me on the right path in Zen, but he never criticized my personal character or intelligence, nor did he teach me how to live or conduct myself in life. My calligraphy teacher taught me those things.

Once there was an "Exposition of the Calligraphy of Contemporary Zen Priests" at a department store in Tokyo. Yokoyama Sensei's critique of all the Zen priest's calligraphy was published in a magazine in two installments. There was loud censure. From ancient times it has been said that if you criticize a Zen Master you will fall into Hell; yet, he criticized them mercilessly. I don't think that there was one living Zen Master who was not scathingly denounced.

Because his criticism was so severe, I suggested that he tone it down a little. He responded, "Aside from this, what do I have? Are you telling me to die?" Through calligraphy, he wanted to purify the world; he felt this was his mission.

At one time I thought of terminating my lessons with him because he lacked common sense and because his criticism of my calligraphy was too severe. But as I grow older, I feel very thankful that he did that. Also, thanks to him, I have been able to develop an "eye" for calligraphy. I can look at my own calligrahy and judge it. That is why, in one way, I think that I was saved by Yokoyama Sensei.

Yokoyama Sensei died in 1966 at the age of 83.[16]

While Omori Roshi was absorbed in *Kendo*, *zazen*, and *Hitsuzendo*, a friend told him one day that Yamada Sensei had said, "Although *Kendo* alone is a great enterprise that cannot be mastered in a lifetime, Omori practices *zazen* and calligraphy. In the end, he will fail in all of them." This disturbed Omori Roshi so he went to Seki Seisetsu to to ask him what he should do.

Seisetsu Roshi didn't say that it was good or bad. He said, "A man named Yamaoka Tesshu (1836-1888) got up at four in the morning and did *Kendo*. During the day, he practiced *Shodo* (calligraphy). At night, he did *zazen*. In this way, he was able to do *zazen*, *Shodo* and *Kendo*."

I said, "Well, I, too, will turn everything into *zazen*. *Kendo* will be *zazen*; *Shodo* will be *zazen*; I will do everything as if I were doing *zazen*."

Seisetsu Roshi replied, "Yes, that should do. Give it a try." Even though Yamada Sensei told me to stop, I didn't but did everything as if I were doing *zazen*. Standing *zazen* was *Kendo*. Holding the brush became writing *zazen*.[17]

Zen, *Kendo*, and *Hitsuzendo* were the pillars of Omori Roshi's *shugyo*. *Shugyo* refers to the deepest possible spiritual training. The Japanese language has six words to describe different levels of training: *keiko, renshu, kunren, tanren, kufu,* and *shugyo*. The first four of these perhaps can be translated as practice, training, discipline, and forging, but there are no English equivalents for *kufu* and *shugyo*. In Zen these two terms are closely linked. Daisetz Suzuki explains:

The kufu is altogether personal and individualistic, it is to develop out of oneself, within one's own inner life. Kufu literally means "to strive," "to wrestle," "to try to find the way out," or, in Christian terms, "to pray incessantly for God's help." Psychologically speaking, it is to remove all the inhibitions there are, intellectual as well as affective or emotional, and to bring out what is stored in the unconscious and let it work itself out quite independently of any kind of interfering consciousness. The kufu, therefore, will be directed toward how to remove inhibitions, though not analytically. If such an expression is permissible, let us say the kufu is to be conatively carried out—a process involving one's whole person; that is to say, it is to be totalistic, growing out of the depths of one's own being.[18]

Zen…generally uses the term kufu (kung-fu in Chinese) which is synonymous with "discipline" or "training" (shugyo; hsiu-hsing).

> *Kufu...means "employing oneself assiduously to discover the way to the objective."*[19]
>
> *It is one of the most significant words used in connection with Zen and also in the fields of mental and spiritual discipline. Generally, it means "to seek the way out of a dilemna," or "to struggle to pass through a blind alley." A dilemna or a blind alley may sound somewhat intellectual, but the fact is that this is where the intellect can go no further, having come to its limit, but an inner urge still pushes one somehow to go beyond. As the intellect is powerless, we may enlist the aid of the will; but mere will, however pressing, is unable to break through the impasse. The will is closer to fundamentals than the intellect, but it is still on the surface of consciousness. One must go deeper yet, but how? This "how" is kufu. No teaching, no help from the outside is of any use. The solution must come from the inmost. One must keep on knocking at the door until all that makes one feel an individual being crumbles away. That is, when the ego finally surrenders itself, it finds itself.*[20]

Through his *shugyo* in Zen, *Kendo*, and *Hitsuzendo*, Omori Roshi forged the strength of character which saw him through the turmoil of World War II and extreme hardships in its aftermath.

CHAPTER 2

Renma

Renma: forging and polishing one's character,
like making iron ore into a sword.

1934 – 1945

Jikishin Dojo

In the 1920's and 30's social conditions throughout the world were very unstable. Within Japan, there was the 1923 Great Kanto Earthquake, the subsequent financial panic, and then the dispatch of troops to China. In 1929 the stock market crash in New York caused financial crises around the world. In Japan many Communists were arrested; Prime Minister Hamaguchi was assassinated and the agricultural depression, which became more and more serious, was accompanied by widespread anxiety.

In 1931, there was the outbreak of the Manchurian Incident. The army made two unsuccessful *coups d'etat* in March and October, 1931. Prime Minister Inukai was assassinated in May, 1932. Japan withdrew from the League of Nations in 1933. Political conditions within and without Japan became increasingly unstable. Whether he wanted to or not, Omori Roshi became caught up in the whirlwind and in July of 1933, was involved in the Shinpei Group Incident, another attempted *coup d'etat*. Omori Roshi recalls:

> One of the leaders of this incident, Mr. Suzuki, asked me to join them. But after listening to what he said, there were several points that I could not agree with. One of their targets was General Araki, a man that I respected. At that time, the army was divided into two factions. General Araki's faction was trying to end the Manchurian Incident as soon as possible. The other faction planned to occupy northern China and wanted to force a less militaristic general like Araki to resign. Their aim was to replace him with General Hayashi, who was the commander in Northern China.
>
> The leader of the Shinpei Group was Maeda Torao. Maeda and I discussed this at an inn in front of the Meiji Shrine all night. This meant inevitable death. If I agreed, I'd die. If I didn't go along, I'd surely be killed. The time from 7 p.m. till the next

morning seemed like an instant. In the end our discussion fell apart. In the morning, Maeda said, "Let's forget it all," and left. He told me I could do what I wanted.

I wondered why he did that and asked the others, "Can I really go home?" Then I got up and left. But the police were already looking for me as one of the top leaders in the affair. I was on the list of people to arrest. I had to hide, so I left for Nagoya with only the *kimono* I was wearing and my short sword.

In Nagoya I was caught in a police cordon and was searched, but my sword was carefully hidden under my arm. The detective did not find it. He told me to show him all of my belongings. Feigning ignorance, I took out my towel and wallet. He asked me, "What's your job?"

"A newspaper journalist," I replied.

"What were you doing?"

"I was playing *go*." That is how I passed through the police cordon. From then, I went from place to place and hid. Kuroki Shosa had a summer house at the foot of Mt. Fuji so I stayed there awhile.[1]

In 1934, when he was 30, Omori Roshi founded the Jikishin Dojo in Koishikawa. He describes the beginning of the Jikishin Dojo below.

I was favored by Kuroki Shosa, whose dream was to create a utopia in central Asia. Kuroki told me, "Please develop the young men who will come with me." That's why I created the Jikishin Dojo. I built it with my own money, but Mr. Kuroki gave me tremendous support. Live-in students came and went, but there were always around 30. Due to illness, however, Kuroki died later that year and did not realize his dream. After Mr. Kuroki passed away, Shiga Naomasa and Kobayashi Junichiro supported the Dojo.

When I created the Jikishin Dojo, I asked Ryusuke Sensei to be the chief advisor for our Dojo. He said, "I can never practice martial arts. But if you really want me as an advisor, please get my father's approval since he is taking care of me."

I went to ask Toyama Mitsuru and explained the circumstances. He said just one thing, "My son's body is sleeping, but his spirit is not." I took it to be Mr. Toyama's way of giving his approval and went to Ryusuke Sensei right away.

When I told him what his father had said, he said, "You are a strange person to want this stupid eldest son of the Toyama family," and laughed.

When I told Mr. Toyama that the Dojo would have Ryusuke Sensei as chief advisor, he smiled and said, "I cannot help you financially, but I will write some calligraphy for you." Then he added, "If no one comes after you build your Dojo, swing your bamboo sword by yourself. No one need come. Train by yourself. Since ancient times, there has never been a person who starved from doing the right thing. If you are doing what is right, *Ten* (Heaven, God, Nature) will surely provide food. But even if this were not so, you be the first who starves and dies from doing the right thing." Those were very severe words.[2]

Nakazawa Museki, the first student of the Dojo, described the training as follows. "One day every month at dawn, we went to worship at Meiji Shrine, a distance of 16 kilometers round-trip on foot. On regular days we were awakened at 6 a.m. by Omori Roshi and cleaned the Dojo. As we finished one by one, we went into the martial arts Dojo and sat in meditation for the duration of one incense stick (about 45 minutes). Then we chanted a *Shinto* prayer. Every afternoon from 4 there was *Kendo* and *Judo* practice. On Monday, Wednesday, and Friday, at 5 p.m., we took turns reading and explaining books. On Saturday evenings there were relaxed, informal meetings. From the 15th of every month for five days, there was *sesshin*. During *sesshin* from 4 in the morning till 10 at night, we trained diligently."

For Omori Roshi the arts were a way of realizing Zen with the the body and expressing the realization in activity. He wrote:

A martial way whose purpose is learning techniques or winning at sporting matches has no value in itself. Its only value is as a means of attaining something outside itself, such as a strong body, courage, or enthusiasm. If one calls this a martial Way, then the way will become of secondary significance. But essentially martial Ways are not that. As a way of human being, the Way in itself has value as a dignified first principle.

If you understand *Bushido* as only "Hurry up and die," then this is simple-mindedness or defeatism. For me, in the deeper meaning of these words, I seem to hear the teachings of Dogen Zenji, "To study Buddhism is to study yourself; to study yourself is to forget yourself." Also, "Just forget, set your mind and body free, and throw it into the house of the Buddha (which here stands for life, whole, void). In *Bushido*, as a traditional Way transmitted from ancient times, a person throws his mind and body into *Bushido*. Forgetting himself and becoming one with the Way, he completely transforms the small self into the Way of the warrior. He then lives the Great Life.

Omori Roshi in front of the Jikishin Dojo (1934).

Omori Roshi reading sutra *(above) and demonstrating a sword* kata *(below) in the Jikishin Dojo.*

In this politically turbulent period of Japanese and world history, the Jikishin Dojo became the headquarters for the People's Movement. According to Nakazawa, the Jikishin Dojo was initially committed to rejecting the philosophy that the Emperor was just a part of the government, and to preserving the traditional sacred status of the Emperor. This was part of their efforts to oppose Japan's expansion into China and joining the Triple Alliance with Italy and Germany. The leaders of the Jikishin Dojo believed that this would inevitably draw Japan into a world war that they could not win.

On February 26, 1936, young army officers revolted in an attempt to uphold the supreme command of the Imperial authority. Because of his ties to members of this group, Omori Roshi was arrested and held for two months at the Otsuka Police Station, but they were not able to convict him. He recalls this period.

> The prosecuting attorney said that I had agitated the Emperor's army. I asked, "Do you really think that an ordinary citizen like myself could agitate the soldiers of the Emperor? If you think that, you are really showing contempt for the army." When I said that, the prosecuting attorney began to tremble. I continued, "During the February 26 Incident, you called them (those who participated in the incident) revolutionary soldiers, in other words, you were calling them the enemy. If that is so, according to military law, in the event that the general staff office is occupied by enemy forces, even if just temporarily, the person in charge must be punished. Was the commander in chief, Kaninnomiya (an aristocrat) punished? If he has not yet been punished, he should be punished before me." When I said that, the prosecutor's face turned blue.
>
> During the February incident, the persons involved in the incident had come to me for advice, but I said, "Now is not the time. You must wait a little longer," and opposed the action.

In 1937, Kuroda Sueo, a student of Omori Roshi, posted flyers opposing military agression in China, and Omori Roshi was incarcerated in Sugamo Prison for one year for donating money to Kuroda. After a year in prison, he was on probation for three years, but in 1940 he was pardoned and his record cleared. He relates his experiences in prison.

Among the prisoners, one who had relatively good behavior served the meals. He served *miso* soup into a bowl which was on a tray. When he came to me, while keeping an eye out for the guards, he would pour the soup until it overflowed. Though I would say, "That's enough," he would always fill the dish to the brim. Since I am a small eater, I could not possibly eat it all and threw the left-over into the toilet of my solitary cell. At first I thought that the person in charge wanted to be nasty, but he acted so strangely when he served the food that when I thought about it, I realized that he was trying to be kind to me. He thought that I would be hungry so he gave me a lot. I didn't know what to do.

One day a guard asked me, "Sensei, would you like to read books?"

I said, "Yes, I would but I don't know how to go about it."

He said, "You must call me and say, 'I would like to see the chaplain.' Then the chaplain will come and you can ask for a list of the books available. If you write the name of the book that you wish to read on this board, you will get the books that you need." Saying this, he returned to his place.

Right away I called, "Guard. Guard."

The same guard came to my cell and said, "What is it?"

"I would like to see the chaplain," I said. He went to call the chaplain. I did as I had been told. Eventually, I read all the books on philosophy and religion that they had in the prison.

Whenever I would read the books, I would note the important points in my head. When I wrote my weekly post card, I would write these main points and send the post card. All the knowledge that I presently have is based on the books that I read while I was in prison.

A guard once said to me, "If you only read those difficult books, even if you are released, you will return here. You must read less serious books."

I asked him, "Then, what kind of books should I read?"

He said, "Novels should be good." Therefore, I read the complete works of Natsume Soseki.

A solitary cell in a prison is a great convenience. Everything can be done in one room: the toilet is there; you can eat there; you can even study there. While I was there, I didn't think that I should read all the time, so during the day I read books, and at night I did *zazen*.

The day I left the prison and returned to the Dojo, Seisetsu Roshi came for a visit and said, "You had a long *sesshin*. You had much hardship, but you did well." That night, he took me to dinner. Since there is no other place where one can study so leisurely, everyone should do the right thing and get into prison.[3]

In 1938, Roshi married Yoshie Yamashita. He met her through her mother who had also trained in *zazen* with Maeno Jisui to improve her health. Later when Roshi began *sanzen* with Seki Seisetsu, he would sometimes stop at their family home in Shizuoka on his way back from *sesshin*. After Yoshie began school in Tokyo, they gradually became acquainted. Her father, however, was adamantly against their marriage saying, "I can't give my daughter in marriage to that *ronin* (masterless *samurai*)." Omori Roshi did not have a job like most people did and never knew when he would lose his life. One day after they had married, however, Mrs. Omori's father went to the Dojo in Setagaya. He was received by Roshi's students with such courtesy that he was deeply moved. From then on, he recognized their marriage. Mrs. Omori's younger brother also respected Roshi very much and became his student.

Also in 1938, the Jikishin Dojo moved to Setagaya onto an estate of about 1.6 acres rented from Tamaki Bunnoshin, the successor of General Nogi of the Meiji era. Roshi's wife shares a recollection of that time, "It was a very big place. Our residence was connected to the Dojo by a long corridor. For some reason, perhaps it was because there were always many students in the Dojo, Roshi never locked the doors. Because of that, I was terrified being alone in the house. The place where the students were and where we lived were very far apart. In addition, Roshi went all over Japan giving lectures so he was rarely at home."

Omori Roshi not only taught his students but also supported them financially.

> Support was furnished by Mr. Shiga. I, however, taught *Kendo* here and there. For example, I taught at the Konan Training School which trained the commissioners for the Southern Region. The salary was very high. From teaching at various places, my monthly income was about 1,000 yen. Of this, 300 yen was required to cover the expenses of the 30 live-in students. Actually, even without Mr. Shiga's contribution, I could have supported my students. I also paid the schooling expenses of some of the 30 students. This continued until the end of the war.

Despite leading the Jikishin Dojo, Omori Roshi continued to go to Kyoto every month to attend *sesshin*. In 1939 Seki Seisetsu, with whom Omori Roshi had been doing *sanzen*, became the *Kancho* (Archbishop) of Tenryu-ji, and left his position as the *Shike* (Abbot) of the monastery. Seki Bokuo, who had finished his training and was the head priest at Tojiin, became the *Shike* of the monastery and conducted *sanzen*. For ten years, from that time until he became the priest at Kohoin, Omori Roshi did *sanzen* with Bokuo Roshi.

After the February 26 Incident, the outbreak of the Sino-Japanese War, and the formation of the Axis powers, Japan was slipping increasingly faster into world war. In 1940, at the age of 36, Omori Roshi tried to prevent Japan's involvement in World War II. He recalled with gravity and deep feeling:

If I hadn't been so weak, I might have been able to prevent the war. I deeply regret this.

When they were planning for the second Konoe cabinet, I went to Karuizawa to meet with Mr. Konoe (*Kanpaku* or chief advisor to the Emperor). I went everyday but was never able to get an appointment. Since everyone thought that Konoe would become the next prime minister, politicians were visiting his country home everyday.

At that time, the governor of Nagano Prefecture (where Karuizawa is located) was Tomita. From the hotel I called Mr. Tomita and said, "I want to meet Mr. Konoe but haven't been able to. Could you please call him and ask him to meet me?"

In a little while, I got a call from Mr. Tomita who said, "Please go to see Miss Toku tomorrow at 10:00. Then you can meet him." Miss Toku was a very intelligient woman who acted as his secretary.

At 10:00 the next day I went to see Miss Toku and she arranged for us to meet right away. Because of my spiritual weakness, however, I was unable to change his mind. I said, "Mr. Konoe, you will probably be issued an Imperial mandate to form a cabinet."

Konoe replied simply that he was worried about this possibility

"The most important post is that of commander of the army. Whom will you choose for this?" I asked.

"I am thinking of General Ugaki or General Mazaki," he replied.

"I feel the same way," I said. "But the law has been changed. If the appointee is not in active service, he cannot become the commander of the army. Since Generals Ugaki and Mazaki are in the first reserve, they cannot be appointed. What will you do? Will you still choose one of them?"

"That is what is causing me so much headache. I am wondering what to do," he responded.

"*Kanpaku*!" I exclaimed. "There is only one way to do it. When the Imperial mandate arrives, go to the Emperor for help. Get a direct order for the commander of the army from the Emperor. If it is a direct order, it doesn't matter whether they are in the reserves or not. Please ask for a direct order from the Emperor."

"I have been thinking of that, too," he said. "However, it would be hiding behind the skirts of the Emperor, and I can't do that."

I said, "Please hide behind the Emperor's skirt. I know the extreme dilemna you are in as *kanpaku*, but please sacrifice your Konoe family reputation for the sake of Japan. Hide behind the Emperor's skirts and bear the dishonor of being called a traitor. Please ruin your Konoe family. Please crush your family and save Japan. Please, I beg of you."

I repeated it many times, and he replied, "Please leave it to me."

"The only way is to get a direct order from the Emperor. There is absolutely no other way. I am very sorry, but please prepare to sacrifice your family for the sake of Japan and do it." I said that and returned to Tokyo.

In a while, Konoe received the Imperial mandate and returned to Tokyo. After that, I took every opportunity possible to say to Mr. Konoe, "Your Excellency, it's still not too late. Please become a traitor. Please sacrifice your family." When I told him this, he looked very displeased and turned away his face disgustedly. Since I always said the same thing, in the end, he didn't call me anymore (to his advisors' meetings).

At that time, the governor of Nagano prefecture, Mr. Tomita, became the *shokikan* (Mr. Konoe's secretary). Whenever I met him, I said, "Mr. Tomita, please tell Mr. Konoe that Omori said this." Tomita showed more and more displeasure. Because of that, no one called me anymore.

When I think of it now, I was weak of purpose. I should have persisted until the end. If one trains in Zen, one must do everything thoroughly and completely, but in this case, I neglected to do it. I should not have given up. I should have persevered and even used intimidation if necessary. This is the one thing that I regret deeply.[4]

Universal Brotherhood

Although he had tried his best to prevent Japan's involvement in World War II, Omori Roshi was just as determined to see the war through to the end. Winning or losing was not the point. He felt that something that had been started should be carried through to the end:

> Since I wanted to resist till the end, I was going to obstruct the Emperor's broadcast (in which he would announce Japan's surrender). For that reason I often went to the Imperial Headquarters to incite the soldiers. Since Yokoyama Sensei did not know this, he came to my *dojo* in Setagaya and said, "These days all Japanese have become hopeless cowards. Our country has lost, but not one person has come forward to commit *seppuku*. How about it? Let's do it in front of the shrine for General Nogi."
>
> I thought that this was impossible, but since he had said this to me, I thought that I had no other choice but to do it. Yokoyama Sensei asked me, "Do you have a very sharp short sword?" I told him that I had decided to kill myself instantly with a pistol so Sensei said, "If that's the case, let me borrow your short sword."
>
> But I said, "Sensei, if you are going to commit *seppuku*, don't you think that it is dishonorable to kill yourself with someone else's sword?" and did not lend it to him. Then we made a promise to commit *seppuku* and parted. The next morning at

about 4:00, he came and said, "Hello, Hello," and woke me up. He said, "I absolutely believe in Japan's national structure, but Japan has lost the war. The reason we lost the war is because there was some weak point. It is very important that we investigate this thoroughly. I realized that it isn't good to merely commit *seppuku* and die. It won't be too late to die after we completely investigate the reason. What do you think? Let's postpone it." I agreed right away, but if he hadn't come, I would have committed *seppuku*.[5]

In mid-September of 1945, though he knew he would have difficulties with transportation, Omori Roshi went to Kyoto to seek guidance for the future from Seisetsu Roshi. Since the war had just ended, everything was still in confusion. There were few trains, none of which were running on a regular schedule.

At that time, Seisetsu Roshi was critically ill and not seeing anyone. Since there was nothing I could do, I left a little something as a get well gift and started to leave. When I got to Shogan-ji, which is on the grounds of Tenryu-ji, the *inji* (Roshi's attendant) came running after me and said, "If you are Mr. Omori of Tokyo, Roshi says that by all means he would like to see you." When I went back, Roshi had gotten up and was sitting up with his two elbows leaning on a small desk.

He asked me question after question such as, "What will happen in the world from now? What should Japan do?" I didn't know the answers. That was the reason that I had come all the way from Tokyo to see him. But I couldn't answer that I didn't know. After training with him in *sanzen* for so long, if he asked me a question, I felt that I had to give him an answer.

Immediately I felt as if we were in *sanzen*, and I answered seriously. Roshi then called his *inji* and said, "Bring some whiskey." When the *inji* brought a bottle, Seisetsu Roshi said, "No, no, not that. Bring the other one." This happened several times.

Finally he said, "Bring the best one!" The *inji* brought Old Parr and exchanged the drinking cups that he had brought for gold ones. Roshi himself poured me a drink.

I had one drink and tried to give the cup to Roshi so that he could drink, but he said, "Since I am in this condition, I cannot drink. You drink in my place." After I had had several drinks, he straightened his posture and said, "This is what I think." He told me his thoughts and at the end, he said, "There are many cabinet ministers and many generals whom I have met, but there is not one person who truly understands the spirit of *Hakko Ichiu* (universal brotherhood). This is not good. In order for Japan to recover, I think that during the next six months it is necessary for someone to drum the true meaning of *Hakko Ichiu* into the hearts of all Japanese people. If I were in good health, I would like to do that. You are a patriot. Now is not the time to be idly doing *zazen*. I urge you; please do this in my place. If I get better, I will join you. Until then, please do this for me." While he was saying this, he held my hand tightly.[6]

On October 2 of the same year, at the age of sixty-eight, Seisetsu Roshi passed away. His last words, "Teach the spirit of universal brotherhood," became his dying wish to Omori Roshi. Believing in this and carrying out Seisetsu's Roshi wish became Omori Roshi's lifetime task.

Hakko Ichiu was a phrase often used during the war. Its real meaning is that, from the beginning, everything and everyone has Buddha nature, and that with this view as a base, all people of the world can create "One World" peacefully.

I was not there when Seisetsu Roshi died. When the end came in September of 1945, he called Bokuo Roshi and said, "I don't have much longer to live. I will die soon."

Since Bokuo Roshi is the kind of person who insensitively says anything without thinking, he told Seisetsu Roshi, "Roshi, please die tomorrow (September 30). Then we can read the *sutra* for you at the memorial service for our founder (Muso Kokushi). We can kill two birds with one stone. We will have to read the *sutra* only once."

Smiling wryly, Seisetsu Roshi said, "Well, that probably won't happen."

"But, please try to die tomorrow," Bokuo Roshi persisted.

Seisetsu Roshi, however, did not die on the 30th. On October 1, he said, "When I raise my hand, start chanting *Shiku Seigan* (The Four Vows of the Bodhisattva). Then, at the end, when you hit the *inkin* (small hand-held bell), I will stop breathing. Please do that." Yamada Mumon Roshi and two others were at his bedside. When Seisetsu Roshi raised his hand, they began chanting, "*Shujo muhen sei gan do...*" and at the end hit the *inkin*. When they did that, the doctor came flying in and gave Roshi an injection to stimulate his heart.

Then, Seisetsu Roshi said, "Not today." He added, "Tomorrow, when I raise my hand, you must not give me an injection," and he forbade the doctor to give him a shot. On the night of October 2 when he raised his hand, they recited the *Shiku Seigan sutra*. The *inkin* was hit—"*Chiinnn*"—and he said, "*Aaaaah*," with a big yawn and breathed his last breath. This was truly a magnificent last moment.[7]

After the war because times were hard, the Tamaki's had to sell the Jikishin Dojo property. Notification of the dissolution of the association was filed, and the Jikishin Dojo disappeared legally in August of 1945. In 1946 Roshi and his family went to live at Toji-in in Kyoto.

CHAPTER 3

Gogo no Shugyo

Gogo no shugyo: endless refinement to totally live one's enlightenment.

1945 – 1994

Seki Bokuo

Seki Bokuo Roshi was the priest at Toji-in, living there with his wife, when Omori Roshi and his family moved into the guest room. In 1946, following the death of Seisetsu Roshi, Bokuo Roshi was nominated to be the next Archbishop at Tenryu-ji.

Seki Bokuo, whose formal name was Shitta Shitsu, was born in Guma prefecture on April 15, 1903. In 1923 he entered Keio Medical school but withdrew after a few years. He was interested in the ideology of Mushanokoji Saneatsu's "New Village," which was a utopian community promoting ultra-individualism and lived there for several years. In 1928, he became a student of Okabe Koju of Zuigan-ji in Gifu prefecture and entered Myoshin-ji, but had to return to Zuigan-ji because of illness. In 1930, he entered Tenryu-ji. In 1937, he was appointed by Seisetsu Roshi to be the priest of Toji-in. In 1939, he became the *Shike* (Zen master in charge of training) of Tenryu-ji. From 1946, until his death in 1991, he was the Archbishop of Tenryu-ji.

During his monastic training, Bokuo Roshi pushed himself severely. After the regular formal sitting, he sat in *zazen* from the 9:00 "lights out time," till 12:00 and never missed a night.

He could only sit in the half lotus position. Since one of his knees would not go down to the cushion, he put a rock on it. For that reason, in his later years, he suffered from backaches. Unless you experience this yourself, you cannot imagine how painful it is. To continue this kind of training is very difficult, but he trained relentlessly.

He went through his *koan* training so quickly that his teacher, Seisetsu Roshi said, "It is too fast." In only seven years, he finished training that normally took fifteen to twenty years.

In addition, he was very intelligient. To answer his *koan*, he would present Chinese poems or parts of poems to his teacher. There is a book called *A Zen Forest* in which there are about 5,000 Chinese terms. He memorized this whole book. While doing *zazen*, he would turn the pages in his mind looking for an answer to give to his Zen master.

Omori Roshi would often say this about Bokuo Roshi, "Whenever I heard the answers that he had given to his *koan* or the terms that he used, I always thought, 'It is no wonder that Seisetsu Roshi chose him.'"

He liked everything to be very clean. When he was the priest at Toji-in, Omori Roshi lived with him for awhile and saw this first-hand. He relates, "He was an earnest seeker of the Way and also liked everything to be clean. He especially liked to clean the roof. Holding a bamboo broom, that tall man would climb onto the roof and would sweep. There were many fallen leaves on the roof. If the leaves piled up, the rain gutter would rot. That is why he would go up onto the roof and sweep down the pine leaves."

1971, Seki Bokuo.

As a Zen master Bokuo Roshi's severity was unsurpassed. He says this of himself,

> *Assuming the responsibilities of the former monastery Zen master Seisetsu Roshi, I had to take charge of the training of 20 or so monks. However, after examining the substance of each one, I found that there was not one who was satisfactory.*

> *When they came to sanzen, I hit them so severely that three monks immediately left. Somehow, Seisetsu Roshi heard of this and summoned me. In fear and dread, I went before my teacher. He admonished me carefully and minutely saying, "In order to cultivate your disciples, you must not be quick-tempered. You must have a fatherly attitude that an elderly shepherd feels for his cows or horses. You must have more patience and perseverence than those you train."*

In 1946 at the age of forty-two, Omori Roshi entered the Buddhist priesthood with Seki Bokuo as his teacher. He became a priest of the Tenryu-ji Branch of the Rinzai Zen Sect. Roshi says this about his entrance into the priesthood:

> The first half of my life ended when Japan lost the war. According to the *samurai* code, I became a Buddhist priest.
>
> When I became a priest, I did not know whether it would be all right to have a family or not. I asked Hisamatsu Shinichi for advice. Hisamatsu Sensei, a philosopher, former professor at Kyoto University, and a lay student of Nishida Kitaro, made a big contribution to the Zen world. One of his literary works is *Toyoteki Mu* (The Eastern *Mu*). Altogether, his works encompass eight volumes. I asked him, "Should I separate from my family and become a priest?"
>
> Sensei said, "From ancient times, there have been two ways: as a lay person, one could have a family; as a priest, one had to separate from one's family. But there is another way. That is the 'Great Vehicle (*Mahayana*).' Even if you have a family, it is all right; if you separate from them, it is all right also."
>
> I thought, "Good!" and decided to practice the Great Vehicle.

Omori Roshi left his family at Toji-in and began his life as a Buddhist monk.

> After entering the monastery, I read the Emperor's Imperial Proclamation of the end of the war many times. In accordance

with the Emperor's decision, Japan accepted an unconditional surrender. I pondered why the Emperor chose to end the war. Why did we accept the end of the war? What exactly is our fate from now on?

In the Imperial Proclamation, it is written, *"Banse no tame ni taihei o hiraku"* ("We will open the way for peace for generations to come"). Then I understood why the Emperor resolved to end the war and realized that our job was to carry out the ideal of eternal peace to the world.

As for *sanzen*, Omori Roshi had had a difficult time with his first *koan*, *Mu*, working it for eight years under Seisetsu Roshi. But when he finally broke through this, he passed 20 *sessho* (questions to check whether or not the student really understood the *koan*) at one time. From that time, he passed many *koan* under both Seisetsu and Bokuo Roshi as a lay student. With this background, if he entered the monastery as a full-time monk in the monastery, he could finish in a very short time time.

He stayed at the monastery for about three years. In 1948, Bokuo Roshi told Omori Roshi to become the priest at Koho-in, a small temple in Tokyo.

Koho-in

In November, 1943, Koho-in was founded in Higashi-Nakano, Tokyo, five minutes from Shinjuku. Koho-in was a retreat for Seki Seisetsu when he visited Tokyo, but formerly it was the place where Yamaoka Tesshu Koji once had a home. The property had been donated by one of Seisetsu Roshi's students. Omori Roshi had these first impressions of Koho-in:

I was invited to the opening ceremony as a lay person and never thought that one day I would be living there. The gateway entrance was about 120 yards away from the main building. In front of the temple was a lake surrounded by a footpath. On the left was a dense pine forest. In front of this pine forest stood Koho-in on a slightly elevated area.

I thought, "This is really a nice place. Can there really be such a place in Tokyo? I would like to stay in such a place for a night." But I never thought that I, myself, would be living there.

The pine forest and a grove of chestnut trees behind it were completely burned down in an air raid in 1944. Koho-in remained only because the lake protected it from the fire.

At the opening ceremony as I walked through the parlor, I noticed a scroll hanging in the alcove. Since it was a little dark, I could not see clearly. I stood there looking at it for awhile. Behind me I heard a voice saying, "It's Jiun Sonja."[1] When I looked up, I saw Seisetsu Roshi standing there, and he added, "If you are going to write calligraphy, you must strive to be at this level."[2]

Although the grounds of Koho-in were large, usually only the caretakers, a married couple, lived here. For some reason the property on which Koho-in stood and the building itself had only been given to Seisetsu Roshi verbally; it had never been formally registered. During the confusion that had occurred during the end of the war, a subordinate of Sasakawa Ryoichi (one of Japan's richest and most influential men) evicted the caretakers and occupied the building and the land. There was no way to get it back so Bokuo Roshi said to Omori Roshi, "You are the only person that can resolve this problem. If you find a way to settle this matter, you can do what you want with Koho-in." Omori Roshi went to Tokyo in accordance with Bokuo Roshi's wish.

He deliberated on this problem and had great difficulty with it. At that time, because Seisetsu Roshi had used Koho-in as a retirement retreat, it was very important to retain the place. Because Roshi had been concentrating on retaining the building, he had forgotten to negotiate for the pond that was right in front of it. In the end, this subordinate of Sasakawa Ryoichi acquired the rights to the lake. Later, he had it filled and sold the land in lots. Thus, Roshi's life in Tokyo began.

> When I came to Tokyo, I got a list of the temple members. Over three hundred names of great men were on the list, including many generals and admirals. Representative of the members were such people as Tokutomi Soho (a famous writer) and the president of Kaizo Publishing Company. Seeing this register, I thought that if I went to read *sutra* at one house a day and received an offering, I could earn a decent livelihood.
>
> When I went to each house, all the generals and admirals were in Sugamo prison for war crimes. Mr. Tokutomi had retired and was living at the foot of Mt. Fuji at his villa on Lake Yamanaka. When I visited the rest, they said, "I only signed because Seisetsu Roshi asked me to." In the end none of the three hundred influential people listed could help me. From that day, I had no means of livelihood.[3]

When he got married, Omori Roshi had warned his wife of his commitment to the advice given him by Toyama Mitsuru and of the hardships life with him might bring:

> When I married at the age of 35, I told my wife that I had been told by a person that I respect absolutely, "Even if you starve and die, do the right thing." I asked her if it was all right with her. She said, "If that's what you say, it can't be helped." Though she was reluctant, I made her consent.
>
> Even though I felt that Mr. Toyama's words were very severe, I have obeyed them to this day. I did not stray from the path. No matter how much money I was offered, if I thought it was wrong, I didn't do it. Even if my life was threatened, I did not comply. We were sometimes so poor that even if we looked all over the house, we could not find one penny. That is how

poor a life I caused my wife to have. At the longest we went for five days to one week without food, but we did not starve. If we drank only water, we could live.[4]

Mrs. Omori recollects, "Even if we emptied every drawer of the chest of drawers, there was not even one forgotten penny. We could not even receive rations. We and the children had very empty stomachs."

Next to the pond which was a step lower than the site of Koho-in was the shack of Shimura Takeshi. He was a student of Daisetz Suzuki. He has since written many books, but this was during the days when he was unknown. On sunny mornings he would see me massaging myself with a cold towel. One day, for no particular reason, he came up to me and asked, "Mr. Omori. Are you a very rich man?"

"Why?" I asked.

"These are hard times when people don't know whether they will be able to eat or not. Yet, everyday, you nonchalantly chop wood and enjoy a leisurely life. You are in an envious position."

"What do you mean living leisurely? I'm doing this because there is nothing else I can do." "That can't be true. That's stupid."

Athough from the outside, it seemed that we were living without any cares at all but, in truth, we were the epitomy of the floundering water bird. Though it seemed that we were happily playing, our feet had to be always moving for us to stay afloat.

During this time the words of Toyama Mitsuru gave me support. I reminded my wife, "You remember what I told you when we got married, don't you? I feel sorry for the children but be prepared." However, strangely enough, a supporter appeared. A friend came and said, "You look as though you are having financial problems. So you don't have money, huh? Then, let's have *sukiyaki*." He went to buy some meat and left some money when he went home. If he had not extended his helping hand, we would have fasted. I already knew we could get along without eating for a week simply because I had had that experience many times before.

If one has a firm objective in life, that kind of thing is nothing. In our case my wife and I could put on *ajirogasa* (a monk's straw hat), go out as begging priests, and make a minimal living. That is why when young people are poor, I tell them, "Don't lose your head. Be calm and stay still. If you can stay still without scurrying around, you will sink to the bottom of the ocean. When your feet touch the bottom, if you push off from the ground, you will automatically come up and float. Until that time, you must endure it."

It is said, "Those who drown are those who grab at straws." Because they grab at straws, they drown all the more. If you don't grab at straws, you will sink quietly. When you reach the bottom, put a little strength into your feet and come up. That is my outlook on life. No matter what, if we have not done anything to be ashamed of, we can sink to any depth.

There is a proverb: "If you are poor, your spirit is impoverished." From my experience, the opposite is true. If your spirit is impoverished, you become poor. If you live like a miser, you will grab at straw or anything. If you do that, you will be poor and will sink (but will not come up). From my own experience in life, I can say that if your spirit does not become impoverished, you will never become poor.

In life, what exactly is poverty? I think poverty is subjective to a great extent. Take clothing, shelter, and food for example. If clothes protect you from the cold, that should be enough; when it is hot, it is all right to be without clothes. As for shelter, we were very lucky to have the temple. It is a small temple, probably the smallest in Japan, but we were blessed because we did not have to pay rent. As for food, if we cultivated one or two *tsubo* (approximately four square yards) and made a garden, we would have enough to eat.

If our spirit is impoverished, however, we worry about appearance and display. Instead of that, you must live in order to fulfill the goal that you, yourself, have chosen to be your objective. If you eat, live, and clothe yourself in order to fulfill your purpose, you will not have to make such an exaggerated fuss and will somehow make ends meet. I did it. I probably caused the children to suffer, but I did not let them die of starvation. Even if you are poor, you can still do that much. Poverty is caused by spiritual poverty.

As long as the spirit is not poor, the heart can be rich. Even if you are only living on bare essentials, you can still feel as if you are living like a king. You must not demean yourself and live in an obscure corner. You can have the vigorous feeling that you are living in the center of the universe. Since I started my training as a layman, I commuted for a long time from Tokyo to Kyoto's Tenryu-ji. I spent nine days out of the month there. But even if there were not one penny in the house, I managed to get the one way fare and could attend *sesshin*. In Kyoto I somehow got the money for the return fare and came home. This effort continued for several years; it can be done. The reason was because my spirit was not impoverished. Had my will become miserable, and had I become a sneaky person; or had I made people feel sorry for me because I had to worry about travelling expenses and how my family would fare while I was away, eventually, no one would have given me the money. I am living, however, without being one cent in debt. That is because I have confidence that I am doing the right thing and because I openly asked for and accepted the money to go to Kyoto. If one is poor in spirit, one becomes sneaky and cannot say what one wants.

I once had a *senpai* (senior) who became the editor-in-chief of a large newspaper. This man came to me asking if he could borrow money. I told him, "You have already borrowed a lot of money from me, haven't you? I don't know how much it is in all, but you always say, 'Lend me, Lend me,' without returning the money once. You ask me to lend you the money, but do you have a means of returning it?"

He said that he could not return the money. I told him, "Then don't you think that it's better to say, 'Give me.' I ask people to give me the money so I have no debts. You can't return the money, and yet you ask me if you can borrow the money so you feel inferior to me, don't you. Even on the phone, your voice sounds depressed. Even when you come, you look pale. From the next time, please ask me to give you the money."

Even though I told him that, he said that it was difficult for him to ask for the money. If you can't return the money then there is no other way but to ask the person to give you the money. Once you say it, afterwards you will feel refreshed. If you can't return it, say "Give me." That is doing what is right. In his case, his spirit had become wretched. I despise a *sempai* who goes to a *kohai* (junior) in an abject manner.

When anyone falls into hard times, they begin to be maudlin in a strange way. When you hang on to a thin thread, your suffering remains; the agony remains as worldly desires arise. If you overcome that, open yourself, accept what comes, and you will suddenly feel light-hearted. That's how it is. If you have nothing, then you can reach out to anything. That is the strongest way, don't you think? In order to do this, it is important to be determined.

In other words, it is important not to be impoverished in spirit. If you have the energy and confidence not to become impoverished, even if you live the poorest life, it won't bother you. Daito Kokushi once said, "As long as you have shoulders, you will have clothes to wear, and as long as you have a mouth, you will have food to eat." Shoulders were made to have clothes hung on them. A mouth was made to eat food. That is what Daito Kokushi said.

Similarly Christ says in Matthew, "And why take ye thought for rainment? Consider the lilies of the field, how they grow; they toil not, neither do they spin."

Even if that is so, and we say "Man is the lord of creation," if all we think of is ourselves, we lose the chance to make other things live. If you are self-centered and if you think that it is all right as long as you have a life of abundance, when you are in need, no one will want to help you—even if he is a friend. Everyday if even in a small way, you try to do something for the world or to help someone, there will be recompense without fail. To expect something in return is wrong. But no matter what we do, compensation follows naturally.

In any case, I overcame adversity in this way. You might say that it is because I am a priest. Even so, there is no doubt that one can live one's life like this. It may be true that if everyone thinks, "they toil not, neither do they spin," it will be the end of the world. It is important, however, to try to have this state of mind everyday. If you can do that, though your living standard may reach rock bottom, your vigor and energy will not decline. You will have a carefree and leisurely disposition, feeling that you are living at the center of the Universe. If you do not have this vigor and energy, you will become a failure in society.

Omori Roshi with his family, 1961.

> Though it is said, "Even if you must buy it, you must have suffering in your youth," there are those who benefit from this suffering and those who do not. Some people lose to their suffering, and they end their lives without using that suffering as nourishment for their development as a human being. Some people, however, can use their suffering to nurture their own inner progress as human beings and become people of great character. How we individually shape our suffering into part of ourselves makes a great difference in the kind of person we become.[5]

Around this time Omori Roshi and his wife had the misfortune of losing their three year old daughter.

> Our daughter got sick after the end of the war when conditions were still terrible. The doctor said that if she got one hundred injections of penicillin, she might recover. She had tuberculin meningitis. In effect, it stemmed from malnutrition. The doctor, however, had never administered one hundred penicillin shots. At that time one injection of penicillin cost about ten thousand yen. No matter who they may have been, after ten shots, no one could continue because of the expense. The doctor did not know whether her brain would return to normal after one hundred shots, but the illness would be in remission.
> I told my wife, "Let them do it."
> "How will you get the money?" she asked.
> "I will raise it somehow. Let her have the injections," I said. In an emergency parents can be determined. For their child's life, they will do anything.
> But my wife said to me, "That may be all right for you, but please think of the other children." In the end, the only thing that we could do was to watch our own child suffer and die before our eyes. After that child died, my wife cried by herself every night for three years. For a parent, there is no sadder thing than to have your own child die before you.[6]

Gogo no Shugyo (1945–1994)

Although he became the priest of Koho-in, Omori Roshi continued to go to the *sesshin* at Tenryuji every month just as before. Mrs. Omori shares this impression, "After coming home from one week of *sesshin*, he was different from when he left. His feet were unsteady, and he staggered. He had lost weight and was very thin. During just one *sesshin*, his face changed totally. That's how seriously he sat in meditation."

1960

Omori Roshi and Nagata Hoju Roshi, successor to Seki Bokuo Roshi at Takuan Zenji's temple, Sukiyo-ji, 1961.

Zen in Modern Society

After he had become the priest at Koho-in, Omori Roshi continued to participate actively in politics. At the request of Mr. Abe, Secretary of the Interior after the war, he worked on the New Japan Anti-Communist League and continued there for twenty years. He also was a magistrate of the Nakano Court of Justice for about twenty years. When the court moved for reconstruction, Omori Roshi was busy with other matters and resigned his post as a magistrate. Below he tells of his experience as a magistrate.

>   After I became the priest at Koho-in, because we never knew from day to day whether we would eat, a lawyer named Fukazawa Sadao probably felt sorry for us. He organized a lecture series for me with the Tokyo Lawyer's Association. That is how the *Hoso Zenwa-kai* (Lawyer's Zen Study Group) began. Once a month I would lecture on Zen to them. Then through the recommendation of the hundred or so lawyers who belonged to this group, I became the Tokyo area judicial magistrate. I guess they wanted to make life easier for me and my family and kindly recommended me for the post. During the 20 years that I was the magistrate for civil cases, I was able to make a thorough study of human beings.
>   I found that the living creatures known as human beings are unable to see things correctly. As a civil mediator, I dealt mainly with debtor\creditor cases involving money, land, and homes. There were many complications in these cases, and everyone had things that they wanted to say. The simple truth, however, was that something had been borrowed or rented. Moreover, public and private documents proved the truth of what had been exchanged, and I could not understand why people did not understand the facts as they were. There were even cases where one side said that something was round, but the other side said that it was square. In her book *The Logic of Listening*, Fukunaga

Mitsuko of The International Christian University highlights people's inability to see truth by describing an experiment she carried out.

Fukunaga took 27 university students to the woods in Musashino. She told the students to record any and all sounds that they heard during a ten minute period. Returning to the classroom, she had every student read their list one by one while the other students listened. Some students laughed; some students were surprised. She had each student write their conclusions about the exercise. Here are a few of them:

1. *People expressed the same sound differently.*
2. *Others thought they had heard sounds that they had not.*
3. *Though they thought that they had concentrated hard and had heard everything without missing anything, they had, in fact, missed some sounds.*

Fukunaga took the 27 students to the forest again and gave each a leaf. All the leaves were of the same species. They were told to observe the leaf for ten minutes. Then she had them write down what they had touched and seen. In the classroom each student read out their impressions. The following is a sample of their conclusions:

1. *It was difficult to express what they had seen and felt.*
2. *Each person's impression was different.*
3. *Some people saw things that others didn't notice.*
4. *Some felt things that others didn't feel.*
5. *They thought that they had seen everything but obviously they could not have seen everything.*
6. *They thought that they had felt everything, but that was impossible.*
7. *They did not have the ability to write down everything.*

After two weeks when the students were asked to write their thoughts on these experiments, almost all of the students wrote that they had learned modesty. In Dr. Fukunaga's opinion:

What the students saw was just a part of that thing. The sounds that they heard were not all the sounds. Further, what they felt was just part of that thing....It is man's fate that he can have only partial knowledge. The reason is that we experience what is happening around us as sight, sound, and touch. Messages are transmitted to the nervous system through our eyes, ears, and skin. When our nervous system is stimulated, we choose what to process. In short, we take in information not as a whole but in parts. The rest, we throw away. We select what to process and what not to. This selection occurs completely automatically and totally unconsciously.

Since I was still a mediator when I read this, I had a great interest in it. Though the students did their best to concentrate, they were born like all of us with a nervous system that automatically and unconsciously makes selections. That is why seeing and hearing can only be accomplished in parts. That is our fate.

Mediation is a confrontation between A and B; it is a serious matter involving profit and loss. Here one concentrates very hard not for the sake of recognizing the truth but to protect one's interests. The objective is to win one's claim. The basis for the selection is not just unconscious. I think that there is something like the consciousness of the unconscious.[7]

In 1958, Roshi's book, *Ken to Zen*, was published by the Chuo Bukkyo Company and was highly praised by Daisetz Suzuki. In a letter to one of Omori Roshi's students, Suzuki wrote:

I was enthralled by Mr. Omori's Ken to Zen. I have Harigaya's book, too, but I had been reading "Harigaya" as "Hariya." I learned through Mr. Omori's book that the reading was "Harigaya." I really believe that

> *ainuke (mutual passing) is the greatest feat in Kendo. I wrote that in my book. Ainuke truly manifests the essence of Kendo.*
>
> *I completely agree with Mr. Omori on the contrast and the harmony between Miyamoto Musashi's Iwao (huge boulder) and the Yagyu style's Marubashi (round bridge). "Ten" (changing, turning, shifting) and "yu" (deep and remote, quiet, dim); "happiness and sadness" and "no happiness, no sadness," between these terms, there are harmony and interpenetration. With this, for the first time, we can speak of Ken and Zen as one. Because I believe that the foundation of the Eastern thought is in Marubashi's explanation, the philosophy of the Absolute Now, I mentioned it in my latest work. If one were to systematize this explanation, it would be the Flower Ornament Sutra.*
>
> *Please convey my gratitude to Mr. Omori.*

Omori Roshi appreciated Suzuki Sensei's review of his book and said in response:

> Daisetz Suzuki Sensei was very kind and highly praised my book on the point that this book was at the foundation of Eastern and Western thought. It seems that Suzuki Sensei showed special interest in *ainuke* ("mutual passing," a *Kendo* term that refers to the highest level of the art when two masters confront each other) and felt that it would be a good way to explain the Way to Westerners. He used my explanation as a reference in the second printing of his *Zen and Japanese Culture*. When I received his excellent book, I found that he had devoted many pages to *Kendo* and Zen.
>
> Harigaya Sekiun created the term *ainuke* to describe this condition attained through the sword. It is the world of absolute peace that transcends winning and losing. It is in a different dimension from *aiuchi* (mutual killing or hitting). We should consider it a cultural treasure left by a man of ancient times. We must try to adapt this concept to contemporary times and build

a peaceful co-existence which is based on the philosophy of this great scholar, Daisetz Suzuki.

In Zen training if you think everything is dualistic (self and other), there will be tension, and you will never be able to achieve enlightenment. You must transcend dualism and enter the realm of *ainuke*. But there is a problem. It is no good just to intellectualise about this realm of *ainuke*. This is a very important point. If you do not have the background and strength of *aiuchi*, you cannot enter the realm of *ainuke*. Your Zen will be empty. If you have not mastered *aiuchi*, it is impossible to learn *ainuke*.[8]

From this time on, Omori Roshi and Daisetz Suzuki became friends. During his later years Suzuki thought very highly of Roshi and felt that his ideas and activities would become influential. When a high government official, concerned about the future of the Imperial family and the Japanese people, hoped that the Crown Prince would go to *sanzen*, he sought recommendations for a teacher. Suzuki Sensei told him, "Mr. Omori would be the best."

1964

Gogo no Shugyo (1945–1994)

In 1964 Suzuki wrote the preface to Roshi's book, *Lectures on the Record of Rinzai*.[9] Here is an excerpt from that preface:

The Record of Rinzai is a book that should be regarded as one of the greatest analects of the Orient—no, of the whole world. I, myself, believe that a book such as Rinzai's, that has so adequately, so delightfully, and, in such a lively manner, presented MU NO SHINJIN (the True Man without Rank), is rare in this world. Even compared to the Zen writings of the T'ang dynasty, this book is a rare masterpiece on this point. Rinzai says, "Take my point of view, and you'll cut off the heads of the Sambhogakaya and Nirmanakaya Buddhas; a bodhisattva who has attained the completed mind of the tenth stage will be like a mere hireling; a bodhisattava of Approximate Enlightmenment or of Marvelous Enlightenment will be like a pilloried prisoner; an arhat and a pratyeka-buddha will be like privy filth; Bodhi and Nirvana will be like hitching-posts for asses." Rinzai is truly a man without rank....Reading Mr. Omori Sogen's most recent work, I thought that even at this late time, I found that someone else thinks the same way as I do. That is why I am relating my thoughts and hope that many will read his Lectures on the Record of Rinzai.

In July of 1966 Omori Roshi went to South Vietnam to invite Thich Quang Duc to Japan in order to persuade him to stop his fast. At that time, Nguyen Kao Ky's administration had imprisoned about two thousand Buddhists. Demanding their release, Thich Quang Duc had begun his fast. Below he relates his experience.

> Eighty per cent of the Vietnamese were Buddhists. Thich Quang Duc was their leader. Because his living or dying could alter the fate of Vietnam, the continuation of his fast was a major problem for the government of Nguyen Kao Ky who was oppressing him. For the American government, if anything happened to Thich Quang Duc, the Buddhists would be stirred up. The political situation would become very grave and would

affect the war. To lose this very intelligient and highly respected leader would be a fatal blow to the one existing Buddhist Association of Vietnam. Though they had different reasons, it is the absolute truth that the continuation of his fast would have a disastrous effect on all three parties.

Before going to Vietnam to meet Thich Quang Duc, I went to see Ambassador Emerson of the American Embassy in Japan. I told him, "I am going to Vietnam to meet with Thich Quang Duc. There is a possibility that I will bring him back with me."

He answered in clear and very fluent Japanese, "I have a great interest in this."

I said, "You say that you have such a great interest in this. If I go to Vietnam, I could be imprisoned for being anti-American or for obstructing the war. Please call Vietnam so that I will not be thrown into prison."

He said, "I will call Secretary of State Habib so please meet with him." When I went to meet Mr. Habib, I learned that we had just missed each other. Since they told me that he had just returned to the United States, I met with a young attache and related my business. I thought that I could then meet Thich Quang Duc, but I couldn't meet him.

Knowing that I had tried various ways to meet Thich Quang Duc, the Japanese Ambassador to Vietnam summoned me three times. He scolded me saying, "What is a private citizen like you trying to do here?"

The third time that I was summoned, I said to the Japanese Ambassador, "I paid a visit to Ambassador Emerson before I left Tokyo. When I told him that I was going to Vietnam and might bring Thich Quang Duc back to Japan with me, he told me that he had a great interest in this idea. I even obtained the agreement of Foreign Minister Shiina."

The Ambassador began to shake and asked, "You know Ambassador Emerson?"

"Since I am here by the invitation of Ambassador Emerson, the Americans will give me access to an airplane wherever I go," I responded.

A little frightened, he asked, "You also know Foreign Minister Shiina?"

"When I was young, Mr. Shiina did *sanzen* and was the student of my teacher (Seisetsu Roshi) so I know him well," I said. Upon hearing this, he began to tremble. I thought, "You little bureaucrat!"

When I finally met Thich Quang Duc, I said, "Won't you end your fast and come to Japan? If you wish to come, I officially invite you on behalf of the Japanese Buddhist League."

Omori Roshi with Thich Quang Duc.

Thich Quang Duc told me, "I would like to go to Japan with you now. But because this is the seventieth day of my fast, my body and spirit are weak and I cannot go now."

I said, "Then, won't you stop the fast?"

He said, "I cannot stop now. The people who helped me are imprisoned. As long as those people are not released, I will share their fate." Then he added, "When there is peace in Vietnam, I will go to Japan." With those words, we parted.[10]

In 1970, Omori Roshi was appointed a professor at Hanazono University, a Buddhist university in Kyoto. During this time there was

Roshi with his wife, Yoshie, at Koho-in, 1966 (above). Training at Koho-in, 1966. (right)

unrest at universities all over Japan. Hanazono University was no exception. Along with Ritsumeikan University, it was well known as a base for the students in the Japanese Red Army. Within the university, there was always strife. One student began a hunger strike in the entrance to the university. He said that he would continue his hunger strike until Omori Roshi was brought to the university as a professor. As a result, Roshi became a professor at that university.

At Hanazono University Roshi's class was "The Practice of Zen." The core of the course was *zazen* and lectures on the *Hekiganroku*,[11] one of the oldest Zen records, and the basics of Zen literature, the *Roankyo*[12] and *Shido Bunan Zenji Kana Hogo*.[13] During his lectures, Omori Roshi would often talk of other things but had the ability to return

Gogo no Shugyo (1945–1994)

exactly to the place where he left off. It was as if he would draw his sword from its scabbard, swing it from side to side with perfect mastery, and then put it right back into its scabbard. While he was a professor, he went to the university in Kyoto from Tokyo every Wednesday to give his lecture.

During that time a Wednesday *Zazen* Club had been organized by the university *Kendo* club. Every Wednesday night at Reiun-in on the grounds of Myoshin-ji, with Roshi as the focal point, the group practiced *zazen*, *hitsuzendo*, and then had tea. It would end at 9:00. This organization continued until 1982 when Roshi's term as president ended. At the beginning only the *Kendo* club members attended, but in the end, there were about thirty people going to the sessions. They were from the pep squad, the *Kenpo* club, *Karate* club, "old boy" members of Tesshu-kai and even the general public.

After these sessions Roshi went to eat dinner at Hanazono Hanten, a Chinese restaurant near Hanazono Station. Approximately ten people always accompanied him and ordered the same thing as Roshi: fried rice, *gyoza* (dumplings) and beer. Roshi always treated everyone.

Chozen-ji and Seitai-ji

In 1970 Omori Roshi met Tanouye Tenshin Roshi who later became the successor to Omori Roshi's line of Zen in America. Tanouye Tenshin was born in Hawaii on January 21, 1938. He was the son of immigrants, both from Kumamoto Prefecture in Japan. From childhood he trained in the martial arts and music. At the early age of 15, perhaps due to the influence of his father from whom he learned the significance of the Japanese martial traditions, Tanouye Roshi was consumed by the question of existence. At the age of 17 while at the University of Hawaii, he committed his life to answering this question through the pursuit of the martial arts. Fortunately he happened to hear Daisetz Suzuki lecture on Zen and swordsmanship and felt as though Suzuki Sensei was speaking to him directly. This experience convinced him that his decision to pursue the martial Way was correct. After deciding on the course of his life, he felt that any bonding he had experienced with others, even his own parents, disappeared.

After graduating from college with a degree in music, he taught orchestral and band music in public schools. Later he developed a curriculum for a martial arts program and taught *Kendo*, *Judo*, and Zen at Farrington High School. While working as a music teacher, for ten years, every summer, he travelled to Japan to train in the martial arts, primarily at Keio University where he practiced *Kendo* and *Judo*.

During this period Tanouye Roshi also taught himself to read Chinese and Japanese texts on philosophy and the martial arts. He worked through these texts with dictionaries, one character at a time. He tested his understanding of these texts against his experience in the martial art, going back and forth between the two until meaning and practice coalesced. He trained in a variety of martial arts because he felt that when the time was right, a great teacher would emerge in any one of them. As he trained in these arts, he began to see similar principles between them and to grasp the strategy of war as articulated by Sun-tzu, which he had studied since age 17.

Eventually Tanouye Roshi became disillusioned at the difference between what he had read and was taught about the martial arts and what he saw in Japan. But he continued. He considered taking the test to become a *yamabushi* (a mountain warrior practicing esoteric disciplines) and continuing his search in that realm. At this point his brother-in-law Hideo Ogura and Toyama Mitsuru's grandson Motokazu, who were both Tanouye Roshi's seniors at Keio University, told him that he must meet the last *samurai* in Japan. They made him cancel a trip to Yamagata Prefecture and introduced him to Omori Roshi. Upon meeting, Tanouye Roshi stated his disillusionment with the Japanese martial arts to Omori Roshi. Instead of giving any excuses, Omori Roshi bowed and apologized for the poor state of the Japanese martial arts. He gave Tanouye Roshi his book, *Ken to Zen*, and invited him back for a demonstration of the *Hojo*. From their first meeting Omori Roshi and Tanouye Roshi felt as though they had known each other for a long time. Upon reading *Ken to Zen*, Tanouye Roshi was very impressed because Omori Roshi had already written about the inconsistencies between what was said and done in the field of *Kendo*.

When Omori Roshi demonstrated the *Hojo* to him, Tanouye Roshi saw all the principles of the martial arts clearly embodied within the four forms of the *Hojo*. He asked to be instructed, but only three days remained before he had to return to Hawaii. Omori Roshi, nevertheless, agreed and was astounded when Tanouye Roshi mastered the *Hojo* in three days. It must be remembered, however, that Tanouye Roshi had been training intensively for ten years at the time he met Omori Roshi and was practicing various martial arts 8-10 hours daily. For example, for one week he swung the sword 10,000 times a day like Tsukahara Bokuden (a famous swordsman in Japanese history, 1490-1571).

Omori Roshi says that a man like Tanouye Roshi appears once in every four or five hundred years and compares him to Saigo Takamori, the Japanese national hero who led the forces of the Meiji Restoration. Omori Roshi describes Tanouye Roshi's *kan* (intuitive perception) as "*surudoi*" (cutting, severe, penetrating) and likens his approach to Zen to Bankei Zenji's. As a Zen master Bankei was a person of immense scale and must have radiated *kiai* (vital energy) so strong that people naturally entered *samadhi* in his presence. He attained this power through tremendously difficult training. Similarly Tanouye Roshi's *kiai* is something which was developed by the severity and intensity of his martial arts training and released through Zen. The problem, however, is that *kiai* cannot be systematized and taught.

After mastering the *Hojo*, Tanouye Roshi realized that there was nothing comparable to *shugyo* (the deepest possible spiritual training) in the West. Because of his background in education, Tanouye Roshi wanted to bring the concept of *shugyo* to the West. He returned the following year with a request to Omori Roshi and presented it in the formal manner of the martial arts tradition:

I told him, "I have a request to make of you."

Omori Roshi said, "What is it?"

I said, "Give me your life for five years."

Omori Roshi asked, "For what reason?"

"There are many reasons," I explained to him, "But basically it is to introduce shugyo to the West."

He agreed.

Circa 1972.

This encounter led Omori Roshi to establish Chozen-ji, International Zen Dojo, in Hawaii in 1972, as "a place of Zen training where persons of any race, creed, or religion who are determined to live in accordance with Buddha Nature (the Inner Self or the Way) may fulfill this need through intensive endeavor." "Chozen-ji" means "the temple of super Zen" or "Zen transcending Zen." Omori Roshi hoped that through Chozen-ji new forms of training would develop which would not be bound by tradition but faithfully transmit the vital essence of Zen to the West.

Chozen-ji had its first home in the band room at Farrington High School where Tanouye Roshi was a band instructor at the time. In August of 1972 Omori Roshi and Kanemaru Sotetsu, a famous Zen cook, came to Hawaii to conduct the first *sesshin*. Stephen Kow, a senior student at Chozen-ji, recalls these days:

Our butsudan was very simple—just a table with a tablecloth, a calligraphy in the form of a circle, an incense burner, and a vase. Kanemaru Roshi had to teach us everything from eating, to reading the sutras, to all of the signals. We used a han (a board which is struck at various times during the day) that Omori Roshi had written characters on. It was made of pine and later shattered by Tanouye Roshi. We had to make do with what we had in those days.

Sesshin was very taxing for everyone. Omori Roshi stayed at a hotel in Waikiki and had to commute every morning and evening to Farrington High School. Since there were no facilities, the food had to be cooked at Tanouye Roshi's house and transported at mealtimes. Martial arts training was done outdoors. There was a strong camaraderie at that time. Everybody suffered during sesshin, and nobody knew quite what to do or expect, but gradually we learned.

In 1973, Chozen-ji moved to a large empty space in the Kukui Marketplace. *Zazen* and martial arts training were held there, but *sesshin* was still held at Farrington High School. In 1974, Chozen-ji moved to a small, rented house in Kalihi. In 1975, Omori Roshi awarded Tanouye Roshi *inka-shomei* to acknowledge his Zen realization. In 1976, Chozen-ji was finally permanently established on two and a half acres of land in Kalihi Valley.

June 1973, With students from Hawaii in front of Koho-in.

Practicing Iaido, *the Way of drawing the sword, 1973.*

1974

In April, 1975, Omori Roshi established another temple, Seitai-ji. Below he talks about his reasons for and the difficulties in starting Seitai-ji.

>Although training laypeople in Zen is worthwhile, these laypeople cannot themselves train others because they have jobs and other commitments. It is difficult for them to teach Zen and assure the continuation of the teaching. Zen priests are needed. To develop such priests and also in order to alter the inefficient aspects of the existing monastic life, I wanted to open a monastery. I looked at many places about one hour away from Tokyo. In the end I decided to open this monastery at Seitai-ji, a temple belonging to Nanzen-ji, in Yamanashi prefecture about two hours away from Tokyo.

I was told that if I went through the *Kaido* ceremony, Nanzen-ji would acknowledge Seitai-ji as a monastery under its jurisdiction. *Kaido* is a ceremony in which one becomes the archbishop of a head temple for a day. One makes one's *dharma* lineage clear and interprets the essence of Zen teaching. In October of 1975, I did *Kaido* at Tenryu-ji and became the archbishop of Tenryu-ji for one day.

After this ceremony I went to Nanzen-ji and said, "I have undergone the ceremony of *Kaido*. Please give your approval of my monastery."

But the administration answered, "We don't remember promising anything like that." This put me in a very difficult situation.

October 1975, Kaido Ceremony at Tenryu-ji, Kyoto.

1975

    I went to Ryutaku-ji in Shizuoka prefecture, Ko-on Monastery in Hachioji, Tokyo, Kogaku Monastery in Yamanashi prefecture, and to others to ask for help. I also called Asahina Sogen, the archbishop of Enkaku-ji in Kamakura. He told me, "Omori-*san*, you do not need the approval. It would be better for you to do it by yourself." Because of the intervention of these monasteries, Nanzen-ji came to inspect Seitai-ji, but they said that they could not give official recognition to a monastery in which lay people and priests train together. Finally, we did not receive their sanction.

I began training under Omori Roshi at Seitai-ji in 1975. Below are some incidents from my time at Seitai-ji.

During *sanzen*, Omori Roshi, who was usually smiling, became a very strict person. When I would enter the *sanzen* room, bow, *sanpai* (a very deep bow), and raise my head, this Roshi who was smaller than most of us seemed like a great mountain.

When Omori Roshi wrote calligraphy and made a mistake, he kept that sheet of paper and practiced characters on the unfilled spaces or drew pictures on it until the sheet was black. Only then did he throw it away.

When he did the cleaning, he wore a sash to keep his *kimono* sleeves out of the way. He dusted the alcove and the frame of the *shoji* (sliding paper door), then got on his hands and knees to clean the floor. He moved the table, swept, and then put the table back. It was like a scaled down general cleaning.

Roshi's favorite television programs were "*Sumo* Digest" and *samurai* movies. When *Sumo* started, he would watch. The *inji* (attendant to the Zen master) had a room close to the Roshi's. When Roshi was at the monastery, the *inji* was always nearby.

While I was *inji*, after *yaza* (evening free sitting), at about 9 pm, I would return to the *inji* room. Roshi would be preparing a manuscript, reading a book, or watching television and having a drink. If he were watching television, sometimes he would knock on my door and say, "Ken-*san*, there is an interesting program on TV. Do you want to watch with me?" When I went to his room, he would bring another glass, and we would drink beer and watch television together. After the program ended, we would talk about training, about our Zen experiences, and many other things. Then I would say "Good night" and return to my room.

This happened during a *sesshin*. I finished *yaza* at about 10:00 and returned to my room. Roshi invited me to watch television with him. I felt very badly about refusing, but I said, "I will continue to do *zazen*."

In a voice that sounded a little lonesome, Roshi said, "I see," and went back to his room. In a little while, Roshi stood in front of my door and said, "I saved a little beer for you so after you finish *zazen*, please drink it."

I went to the kitchen and found half a bottle of beer with a glass next to it. Beside it was a side dish to eat with the beer. He had covered it with a small cloth.

After that, whenever Roshi invited me to drink with him, no matter how busy I was, I always accepted.

During this period Omori Roshi became increasingly busy with a wide variety of obligations. His schedule for a typical month during this period was:

November 1976

1. *Sesshin* starts at Seitai-ji in Yamanashi Prefecture.
2. Return to Tokyo to attend installation ceremony of head priest at Korin-ji.
3. Attend *Kaido* at Myoshin-ji in Kyoto for Kato Ryuho Roshi.
4. Return to Seitai-ji to continue *sesshin*.
6. Lecture at Tokyo Cultural Center. Return to Seitai-ji to close *sesshin*.
7. Return to Tokyo to attend installation ceremony of head priest at Baito-ji. Return to Koho-in to begin Tesshu-kai *sesshin*.
9. Lead memorial service for friend in Tokyo.
11. Close Tesshu-kai *sesshin*.
12. Fly to Fukuoka to attend wedding.
13. Attend wedding and return to Tokyo.
14. Zen training session at Tesshu-kai.
15. Lecture for parents at Meijuro Elementary School.
16. Visit Kubota in Tochigi Prefecture.
20. Morning lecture at Asahi Cultural Center in Tokyo. Afternoon lecture at Zenshoan.
21. Return to Seitai-ji to teach monks.
22. Return to Koho-in.
23. Lecture for high school principals in Tokyo.
25. Lecture for lawyers.
26. Lecture at Asahi Cultural Center.
28. Zen training session at Tesshu-kai.

1979, Demonstrating the opening movement of the Hojo *at Hanazono University.*

Omori Roshi was appointed the president of Hanazono University in 1978. In March of that year, six high ranking Buddhists priests from Kyoto went to Koho-in on an official mission to present a letter from Yamada Mumon Roshi who was then the president of the university and who later became the Abbot of Myoshin-ji. In the letter Yamada Mumon stated that he earnestly hoped that Omori Roshi would succeed him as the president of Hanazono University. Further, it stated that all parties involved had been informed and had accepted Roshi's appointment. All that was now required was Roshi's acceptance. Though Roshi was already the Zen master at Chozen-ji, Seitai-ji and Tesshu-kai and very busy with other commitments, because approval had already been given by all the parties involved, he had no other recourse but to accept the position of president.

Cultural Exchange with Europe

In April of 1978, the French Embassy's Culture Secretary brought Michel Foucault, a distinguished French philosopher, to Seitai-ji, a monastery Omori Roshi founded in 1975. Omori Roshi was attending graduation ceremonies at Hanazono University in Kyoto at that time, so Foucault practiced *zazen* in the meditation hall. When Omori Roshi returned, he spoke with Foucault.

> I did not know what kind of man he was, but the Culture Secretary introduced him as an excellent philosopher of contemporary Europe who surpasses Sartre and said that he had questions that he wanted to ask me. I met Professor Foucault in my room.
>
> Professor Foucault said, "Because my experience has been so brief, I cannot say anything definite. Yet I felt that through the correct posture of *zazen*, I found a new relationship between mind and body. I also felt a new relationship between the body and external circumstances. I have a question regarding the universality of Zen. Is it possible or not possible to separate the practice of Zen from the beliefs and practices of Buddhism in general?"
>
> I responded, "Zen came from Buddhism, therefore, there is a deep relationship between Zen and Buddhism. Zen, however, need not necessarily have the form of Zen. It is all right to discard the name of Zen. Zen is something free. You just said you experienced a new relationship between your mind and body and between your body and external circumstances. To experience this from such short practice is an impressive accomplishment. The experience of the mind and body becoming one and the self and the outside world becoming one are universal experiences. In this sense Zen is international and world-wide. If you just think of Zen as part of Buddhism, this is a narrow,

limited view. If Zen can be understood in the context of your experience, we can fully agree that Zen is universal."

Professor Foucault's second question was, "In Europe, it is thought that Nature and human beings are in opposition. We think that man is the subject which subjugates Nature, and Nature is an object which is ruled by man. Yet according to what I have experienced during the twenty odd days that I have been here, Nature and man are One. Do I misunderstand?"

I couldn't understand all the words entirely but let him pass. Later we pursued this in more detail. As a result, I confirmed that, without a doubt, he had had a realization. That such a respected philosopher would have a realization will be the reason for a qualitative change in the modern civilization of Europe. That he would interpret his realization to mean that man does not conquer Nature but that Nature and man are one is a powerful criticism of modern civilization. That is how the quality of modern civilization will begin to improve. I think that is where Zen is right now. This sense of oneness which Foucault experienced is what Zen can contribute to modern society.

What I fervently hope is precisely what Professor Bernard Phillips of Philadelphia University wrote in his book, *Zen and Western People*:

For the period of at least four hundred years, people in the West have been suffering from spiritual hunger and thirst. When the hope of quenching this hunger and thirst became slimmer because of the inherent religious resources of Western culture, that hunger and thirst became all the more acute....From the traditional concepts that he held on to, man quickly continued to advance toward a united world. Aside from Zen, there is no other universal religion. It is true that many other religions have emphasized a universal religion; but all of the other religions have been influenced by the time, place, and character of the region.

Other religions have been instrumental in a specific nation, during a specific time, and in a specific area. They did not play a part in the lives of all mankind or in all endeavors. They all made the mistake of trying to create an absolute form or absolute creed. The reason is that the forms and creeds of these religions lost their absoluteness and are restricted historically or were the product of a certain geography, certain society, and economic environment. The eyes of modern man are looking to infinity. Because they are always looking at space which unfolds before them without any obstruction, the religion that is so essential to modern man must, like their universe, become a center point that extends everywhere and for which there is no circumference. There is no center point; there is no circumference. The infinite circle has infinite centers.

This practical view is the only thing that has the strength to save people from spiritual hunger and thirst. This practical view, that the center is everywhere and there is no circumference, is the same as the essence of the realization that the Buddha had on December 8, when he was thirty-five years old. He saw the morning star and was awakened to his Original Nature. The center is everywhere and there is no circumference says the same thing as a small particle is the whole; I am the universe itself; the universe is contained in a small particle of dust which is flying around right in front of me in a form which cannot be seen. This way of teaching, this point of view is the principle of *jujimuge* (All things and events in the universe interpenetrate freely without obstruction).

This is the backbone of Zen. The Kegon School's doctrine of cause and condition, and the Tendai School's doctrine of reality are the two facets of Zen. If you can understand what Rinzai meant by "now, in front of your eyes, you, the listener," you will understand Zen completely. At the intersection of space and time is the point where "I" is located. That point is the center of the infinite circle and is located everywhere; there is no circumference. That is reality. This is the basic principle that will save the world.

That is what a foreign philosopher experienced. If one experiences this, modern man's present ideology will naturally be criticized. But by being criticized, change will take place. Without a doubt, this will happen. Just simple theory, however, is not enough. It is necessary to have physical experience behind it. If you experience this, the view that only man is the center of the universe (in exclusion to others also being the center) will become absurd. Why should man alone be the center?

In this doctrine that man is the center of the universe, what is meant by "man?" It is only one's small self or ego. As expected, in subjugating Nature to man's ego, Nature is destroyed; the air is polluted; the ocean is contaminated; chemically manufactured goods are not biodegradable. In other words, the life of the planet will stop. The ecology will be destroyed. How did the world become full of pollution? The source is Man-is-the-center-of-the-Universe-ism which places the single ego at the center. Since the beginning of time, man has not been able to exist independently. Do not think that an independent speck called the ego actually exists. We say, "I, I." But where did this "I" come from? Weren't you born from your parents? I did not make myself and did not come from myself. Where did these parents come from? And, where did their parents come from?

It is the mysterious and fundamental ability of "birth." Through the functioning of this fundamental ability to reproduce, what we call "I" was born. How can this "I" be maintained? We depend upon everything else's energy. This "I" is not able to live at all without carrots, burdock root, fish, meat, and so on. If you have confidence that you can live without the help of anything, we can experiment right now. Cover your nose and mouth with tape, see if you can live for five minutes without the help of air. Do you still insist that you can live without the aid of anything? This is the fundamental mistake of modern man who thought of himself as an independent unit. He paid no attention to the temporal movement of life and the movement of space. He only took the abstraction, the independent unit, "I" which was abstracted from reality. This "I" became the Man-is-the-Center-of-the-Universe-ism. Living like this is what is called man. We are making a terrible mistake on this point. Man is not the center. We are living with the Universe.

1979, Demonstrating the Hojo kata *at the All Japan Demonstration of Traditional Martial Arts.*

I think that it is a tremendous thing that Professor Michel Foucault had such a realization in only 20 days. This realization will perhaps have a culturally historic meaning. Believing this, I set a high value on his experience and feel thankful that he came to Japan to do *zazen*.[14]

1979, Demonstrating the Habiki kata *at the All-Japan Demonstration of Traditional Martial Arts.*

In August of 1979, Omori Roshi headed a spiritual exchange to Europe called "The Fount of East-West Culture." This exchange was conceived in the spring of 1977 after BBC's Trevor Leggett filmed a demonstration of Omori Roshi's *Kendo* and calligraphy. Omori Roshi remarked, "I would like to go to Europe with my *Kendo* sword and calligraphy brush." Father Kadowaki, a Catholic priest who had studied at the Vatican andwho also did *sanzen* with Omori Roshi, took this remark to heart and began making plans. The four facets of the exchange were demonstrations in the martial arts and fine arts, lectures and seminars, visits to monasteries, and first hand experience of Western spiritual training. Accompanied by Tanouye Tenshin as his attendant, Omori Roshi travelled to Europe and demonstrated the *Hojo* and calligraphy in cities in Germany and Belgium. Unfortunately his physical condition did not permit him to finish the tour which went on to include a visit with the Pope.

In October of 1979, after returning from the European tour, Omori Roshi established Chozen-ji as a Daihonzan, the main temple and headquarters of a new line of Zen with Tanouye Roshi as the Abbot. For the canon of Chozen-ji, Omori Roshi wrote:

> Zen is to transcend life and death (all dualism), to truly realize that the entire universe is the "True Human Body," through the discipline of "mind and body in oneness." Miyamoto Niten (Musashi) called it *Iwo no mi* (body of a huge boulder—going through life rolling and turning like a huge boulder); Yagyu Sekishusai named it *Marobashi no michi* (a bridge round like a ball—being in accord with the myriad changes of life). Besides this actual realization there is nothing else.
>
> Zen without the accompanying physical experience is nothing but empty discussion. Martial ways without truly realizing the "Mind" is nothing but beastly behavior. We agree to undertake all of this as the essence of our training.
>
> All our students, strive diligently! Gentlemen of the Rinzai Honzan (Main Temple) in Japan, open your eyes to this and together let us send it out to the world.

1987, Omori Roshi with his wife and the author's family.

    The responsibilites Omori Roshi assumed in his seventies eventually took their toll as he grew older. He was president of Hanazono University, the Abbot of Chozen-ji, Seitai-ji, and Koho-in, and was constantly being asked to lecture. Rarely did he spend more than two days in a row at his home in Koho-in.

    In December of 1988, he suffered a serious stroke, and for the next six years he was bedridden at Koho-in. He had difficulty speaking and remembering, and was cared for by his wife and daughter's family. His condition gradually deteriorated, and on August 18, 1994, Omori Roshi died at about one o'clock in the afternoon. I left Honolulu two days later and visited Koho-in directly upon arriving in Japan. Omori Roshi's body had already been cremated according to his wishes, and the urn containing his ashes and bones, along with a photograph, were set in front of the *butsudan* (altar) in the Dojo. The day before the family had held their private funeral.

    When Zen priests die, traditionally there are two funeral services. One is for the family and relatives; the other is a public service. The public service was held on October 6 at Zensho-an in Tokyo, a temple where he had often taught and where Yamaoka Tesshu is buried. Because Omori Roshi did *Kaido* at Tenryu-ji, and was therefore an Archbishop there, the protocol for the public service was determined by Tenryu-ji. By tradition the invitation for the public service must be written individually and delivered personally. After discussing it with two Zen Masters who were senior students of Omori Roshi, we decided to invite 11 archbishops and Zen masters and 9 Zen priests. There would be 3 *doshi* (priests formally leading and overseeing the service): one head priest and two assistants. Hirata Seko Roshi, the Archbishop of Tenryu-ji, was the head priest. The assistant priests were Kono Daitsu Roshi, the Zen Master of Shofuku-ji and the President of Hanazono University and Koike Shinso Roshi, the Zen Master of Ryuun-in.

After the preparations were finished, the day of the public service arrived. Before the Second World War, as the head of the Jikishin Dojo, Omori Roshi trained many youths, lectured all over Japan and influenced political movements. After the War he was the Zen Master of Koho-in, Tesshukai, Chozen-ji and Seitai-ji. In addition he was a professor and President of Hanazono University. His writings totaled more than 20 volumes, and his lectures and articles were countless. Because of this vast legacy, we were uncertain how many people would attend the service. More than 800 people attended.

As the service began, the invited Zen masters and priests were seated and joined by over 30 other priests. Then cymbals signaled the entrance of the three *doshi*, and the assistant *doshi* read their *kogo* (a Chinese poem). As the assistant priest of Koho-in and also to represent all of Omori Roshi's students, I bowed deeply (*sampai*) before Hirata Roshi and asked him to present his *kogo* as the head priest. His recitation was followed by the chanting of the *Ryogonshu* and the *Shikuseigan Sutra*. As the service neared the end, suddenly a Zen priest came forward and bowed before Hirata Roshi. This was not written in the protocol so I readied myself to jump in to stop the priest if necessary. The priest faced Omori Roshi's picture and said, "We will sing the school song of Hanazono University for you." With this, ten people, both priests and lay people, stood up and started singing to the Roshi's picture. The sound of their voices reverberated throughout Zensho-an and brought tears to the eyes of all.

The 3 *doshi*, more than 50 Zen masters and priests, and more than 800 people devoted more than an hour to the formal, traditional Zen service, but even this could not match the effect of the school song sung by ten people. The school song, offered from the heart, was the real funeral for Omori Roshi. Dedicated to teaching, his life of 90 years was fittingly crowned by a song from the students he had loved like his own children.

After his death, Omori Roshi received the *kaimyo* (official Buddhist name) of "Kaisan Rekijyu Tenryu Tekio Osho Daizenji." Within the *kaimyo* is the accomplishments and lineage of the man: Kaisan means founder of Daihonzan Chozen-ji. Rekijyu Tenryu means he carries the Dharma line of Tenryu-ji. Tekio is his priest name which he used more commonly after 60. Osho means priest, and Daizenji means great Zen master or teacher.

In the "Birth-Death" chapter of *Shobo-genzo*[15] Dogen Zenji writes, "Just set aside your body and mind. Forget about them and throw them into the house of the Buddha. Then all is done by Buddha." When you follow this, you are free from birth-death and become a Buddha without effort or calculation. By this negation of the egotistical self, the life-death of your body functions as the life-death of the Buddha body. Zen without this absolute negation is false Zen or empty Zen. It is not traditional and true Zen.

The life of Omori Roshi is the manifestation of traditional and true Zen. After 8 years of arduous training, he experienced this absolute negation and for the rest of his life tried his best to use his experience of absolute negation in every possible circumstance. He used each hardship as nourishment for his own training and exemplified Shido Bunan Zenji's (1603–1676) words, "If you think of everything as training, your suffering will disappear." Omori Roshi handled the problems in his life by practicing *muga* or No Self. When No Self works through each individual body, the "true Buddha life" or the "blood of the Dharma" is transmitted.

The experience of *muga* is the beginning of real *shugyo*; enlightenment is the entrance to, not the end of, Zen training. Bankei Zenji, a renowned master of the 17th century wrote, "When I was 26 and was doing *sesshin* by myself in Banshu, Akono Nakamura (present day Hyogo prefecture), I was enlightened. I went to see a Chinese Zen master who confirmed my awakening. Now I am 70. The principle which I learned has not changed even a hair since the beginning until now. The clarity of my Dharma eye, however, has totally changed since the time I met with the Chinese master. The Dharma has penetrated my being, and I have attained Absolute Freedom. Please believe me and try your best to perfect your Dharma eye." Bankei explains that the Dharma principle he understood at age 26 when he experienced his great enlightenment, did not change, but only through continued *shugyo* through his whole life, did the essence of the Dharma permeate his being. Only then was he able to move freely. This is the great difference between his youth and old age.

At the end of the *inka-shomei* (the Mind-stamp certificate) in the Tenryu-ji lineage, the Zen master writes, "For now, this is all right. If I were to examine you in more detail, however, you would still have much further to go. Even though your receive the Mind-stamp, you must not become complacent. You must continue your *shugyo*." Even after his death, I believe Omori Roshi will continue his *shugyo* from rebirth to rebirth.

PART II

The Three Arts: Zen - Ken - Sho

CHAPTER 4

Zen and Budo

This chapter is a translation of *Zen to Budo*, an essay by Omori Roshi that was first published in Japan: Daisetz T. Suzuki and Nishitani, eds., Zen, Vol. 5, *Zen and Culture* (Chikuma Shobo, 1968). A more formal translation has already been published, Omori Sogen, *Zen and Budo*, trans. Tenshin Tanouye (Honolulu: Daihonzan Chozen-ji/ International Zen Dojo, 1989).

Budo

In discussing Zen and *Budo*,[1] I wish to take the word *Budo* in a wider sense than simply the various martial arts (*bugei*) and combat techniques (*bujutsu*).[2] The word *Budo* has been used from ancient times to mean more than those. If we look it up in the dictionary, we find *Budo* is described as "the Way to be mastered by the samurai." Again, Yokoyama Kenkichi in his *History of Japanese Budo* states, "*Budo* is the Way of the *bushi* (warrior)."

As I will explain, *Budo* is referred to as *Bunbu Ryodo* (the Way of literary and military arts):

> *Bun* — literally "Letters" and by extension art, culture, civilization and social organization;
> *Bu* — chivalry, martial arts, courage;
> *Ryo* — both, a couple;
> *Do* — a spiritual Way (*Tao* in Chinese).

Budo is therefore never used in the narrow sense of mere fighting arts. If for instance we look at the writings of Nakae Toju (1608–1648), we find a well-known chapter called Bun-bu Mondo (Questions and Answers on Bun-bu) in his work *Okina Mondo*.[3] In his opening statement, he writes, "There is a great misunderstanding about *Bun* and *Bu* among the people at large." He points out that people generally see *Bun* as poetry and cultivated literature in general, together with a softening of the character and a "flowery" aestheticism. On the other hand, archery, riding, military strategy and tactics, and a certain bluntness in character are supposed to be in the realm of *Bu*. Anything remotely cultural is considered to be *Bun*, and similarly, something like straight-forwardness is called *Bu*. Toju points out what a mistake this attitude is.

In Toju's mind, the two form a single ideal (*ittoku*) and cannot be separated; to do so is wrong in itself. *Bun* or culture without *Bu* or strength is no true culture; *Bu* without *Bun* is no true *Bu*. Toju writes:

To govern the nation or country well and to maintain the five fundamental Confucian relationships correctly is Bun.[4] There are some who do not honor the ordinances of Heaven. They are atrocious and have no respect for anything. When they obstruct the Way of Tao, they must be brought to justice and punished. By launching a military campaign against them, those governing re-establish peace for the whole nation. This is called Bu, and in this way Bu forms the basis for Bun.

If we use this interpretation, *Budo* has a wide and profound meaning. In ancient times, men categorized the phenomenal aspects of human life and of all things into two types: *seishin teki* (spiritual and mental), aspects that cannot be seen with the eyes, and the *gutaiteki* (concrete, tangible), the reality which can be seen with the eyes. The former, being passive or hidden, corresponds to *Bun* and the latter, being active or clear, corresponds to *Bu*. But because passivity and activity are integral parts of the whole, *Bun* and *Bu* form one virtue as pointed out by Toju. Hence the Martial Ways that the ancients developed had this same integrated quality.

Hirata Atsutane has written, "The people of our country are innately courageous, righteous and open. These are the qualities of Japan's Yamato spirit, a spirit that seeks great harmony." But because the principles of *Budo* are courage, virtue and straightforwardness, it is more appropriate to refer to *Budo* as *Dotoku*. *Do-toku* is the Japanese reading of *tao-teh*, the first two characters of the Taoist classic *Tao The Ching*, the classic called *The Way and its Power*. *Tao-teh* means that the Way is founded on the martial element.

Often today, the word *Budo* is used mainly in a narrow sense to indicate a specific martial art or technique. For example, *Aiki Budo*, *Judo*, and *Kendo* are looked upon as the representative models of *Budo*. But the reason that the old names of *Kenjutsu* and

Jujutsu were changed to *Kendo* and *Judo* stems from recognition of their qualities as a Way for Man, with profound mental and spiritual significance that goes beyond their methods of combat. For example, it was Kano Jigoro (the founder of *Judo*) who discarded the name of *Jujutsu* for *Judo*. He saw *Judo* as the Way of maximum efficiency in the use of mental as well as physical energy, and it was to lead to the welfare and benefit of all.

In reality, however, the Way is becoming secondary to technique in the martial arts and they are gradually being drawn into the field of sports. The late Yamada Ittokusai in his work *Nippon Kendo-shi* (History of Japanese *Kendo*) marks 21 September 1894 as the end of the era when primary importance was given to the Way. This was the date of death for his *Kendo* teacher, Sakakibara Kenkichi. Ittokusai writes, "After the death of the old master, the reality of the Way will not live up to its name. Many people will not realize this and will simply devote themselves to technical principles. *Kendo* will appear to be popular, but the Way will decline to a very low level." One can sympathize with his feelings of loss.

In the present age, the martial Ways have lost their significance as actual fighting arts. Consequently, it is quite natural that these Ways have been adapted, through necessity, into sports like marathon running, baseball, and swimming. It is essential, however, that the spiritual essence (*seishin*) inherent in the Ways should not be lost.

A martial Way, when practised for a purpose of developing techniques or winning, has no value or aim of its own. Its only purpose is as a device for attaining something "outside" itself such as physical strength, courage or enthusiasm. In other words, if one can call an activity with such purposes a martial Way, then the Way will become of secondary significance. Fundamentally the martial Ways are not a means to attain secondary aims; they are a Way for Man. This in itself is of value as a worthy first principle. If this were not the case, then the

Ways would not be worthy of discussion as a comparison to Zen. It is from this position that I would like to look at the martial Ways.

The Multi-faceted Structure of Human Existence

I have written a book entitled *Ken to Zen* (Zen and Swordsmanship). Simply put, *Kendo* (the Way of swordsmanship) is a method of killing people. Zen is a Way by which man can get rid of his delusions; by becoming enlightened, he may live according to his true self-nature.

Although it is an easy thing to talk about "Zen and Swordsmanship in oneness," what type of relationship is possible between an art for killing people and a Way for man to live? What must one do to bring these two things into unity? The matter cannot be solved by intellect alone, nor can the question be answered merely by words. We could say that this apparently absolute contradiction must be resolved naturally out of one's self, but to actually experience this oneness is not an easy thing. However, no matter how perplexing this problem is, man basically feels a need, or should we say is required, to resolve this apparent paradox.

We really don't know whether tens of thousands of years or millions of years have passed since man first appeared on this planet. But we can say that we have progressed impressively in many ways: ethically and morally, in the development of the Ways, in art, culture and religion, not to mention science and technology. And yet, why is it that, despite a desperate longing for peace, there has not been an interval between wars and conflicts? While possessing nuclear arms that can destroy the world and eradicate humanity in an instant, people go around crying, "Peace! Peace!" What is the hunger these people are expressing?

The *Hagakure* states, "*Bushido* (the Way of the samurai) consists of dying." The meaning here is to pass through (to transcend) death and killing to awaken to the "Great Life." This is the most important issue of human existence and it was this experience that the people of old designated as the purpose of the Martial Ways.

Although this experience does not go beyond the *budoka* (the person who studies the martial ways) himself, its significance in the history of Japanese culture must never be undervalued. These individual experiences have occurred repeatedly through the ages and it is their accumulated effect that enabled the martial arts in Japan to develop into a Way for man.

Baseball, the marathon, and swimming may be said to have their origins in the martial arts. The custom of keeping something of the martial arts alive in the form of sport has been extremely common from ancient to modern times in both the East and West. However, in no other country can we find a full development comparable to the Japanese martial Ways where the way of killing evolved into a Way for man. Unfortunately, the cultural value of this unique evolution has not been recognised and used to create a turning point in world history.

Whether man evolved from an amoeba or his only difference from an ape is the possession of just three more hairs, I really don't know. It is clear, though, that we are certainly not a single-celled organism. Still, we have not become completely independent of the laws of evolution. Because we are part of the evolutionary process, we still have plant-like cells and qualities of wild animals. Layers of physical, biological, and human qualities in a unified structure; this is what we can call Man.

Because of this stratification to his life, man is certainly subject to physical laws, like the laws that govern the world of matter, and biological laws, like those that govern the world of living things. At the same time, there are also the qualities of human character that only man possesses.

But even a man of noble and god-like character cannot live a single day without depriving other forms of life of their life. This is the sad reality of human beings. Even the most honest and compassionate man must snatch water from the earth without paying for it, must breathe the air from the sky without authorization, and must steal energy from the sun. Without these acts, he could not sustain his existence even for an instant. This is the tragic fate of man. Because of this dilemna, everyone bears the original sin of dualism.

Consequently, even if a man really loves peace, he must kill the cow, kill the pig, kill the chicken, kill the fish, and kill the vegetables in order to strive toward this noble aim. To put it paradoxically, this man himself is part of the carnage caused by the survival of the fittest. Therefore, one can say that because there is no peace, he desires peace. Man's existence is subject to this dialectic structure. There can be no human life that does not participate in killing and death. The martial Ways must incorporate this somber fact.

No matter how strong he is, a man thrown into this world will find conflict as long as he possesses animal instincts. His world is the same as that of a tiger or wolf because armed might is no different from the claws and fangs of wild animals. In such a state, the over-riding principle is the instinct of self-preservation. There is no better name for this instinct than that given to it by tradition — *chikusho heiho* (*chikusho* — beastly, animal, brute; and *heiho* — strategy, fighting). As human beings, we can never allow *Budo* to merit such a name.

The World of Play

There are many appraisals of the swordsmanship and character of Miyamoto Musashi. The late Yamada Ittokusai Sensei was quite severe in his criticism:

If he really wanted to test his ability, the swordsmen Shoda and Kimura, both great men of the Yagyu school, were in Edo at that time. There was also Kamiya Denshin of the Shinkage school and Ono Jirozaemon of the Itto school.

It is noted in the *Nippon Kendo Shi* (History of Japanese *Kendo*) that Musashi avoided the strong swordsmen, traveling mainly in the country side and fighting only with those of negligible ability. Nonetheless, because of the explanantion Musashi himself gave at the beginning of his book, *Gorin No Sho* (The Book of Five Rings), I find it difficult to agree with Yamada Sensei's criticism.

Briefly, Musashi said that from the age of 13 to about 28 or 29, he risked his life in dueling about sixty times and did not lose. But around the age of 30, he looked back over his experiences in combat and realized that, although he was victorious in all of his encounters, it was either because the opponent was unskilled or because of accident. He said that by no means did he win because he had attained the highest secrets of swordsmanship. From age 30 onward, he resolved to grasp the principle of the Way.

After a tremendous effort, training day and night, he finally became enlightened to the Way of swordsmanship at about the age of 50. From then on there was no one particular Way through which to continue his training (*shugyo*) other than to spend his time calmly. By means of the principles he had realized in swordsmanship, he was able to master the Ways of various arts and skills although in all these things he did not have a teacher. His writings did not use Buddhism or the teachings of Confucius nor did he use the traditional books on strategy. In doing this he declared that he did not look back at the past.

From this perspective, Musashi had been grasping in the dark before his enlightenment. Frequently, the opponents he beat before reaching age 30 had been weak and that is all we can say. There was a difference in the level of skill and in no way did he win by according with the principles of swordsmanship.

Harigaya Sekiun, roughly a contemporary of Musashi, was the founder of the *Mujushinken Ryu* (the School of the Sword of Non-Abiding Mind). He is known for his criticism of swordsmanship that has one of only three outcomes: 1) victory over an inferior; 2) defeat by a superior; and 3) an equal *aiuchi* (mutual striking or killing). He called them all *chikusho heiho* (animal/beastly tactics). From the perspective of Harigaya's three outcomes, there is no doubt that Musashi was strong, but strength alone without being awakened to the dignity of human nature in the final analysis is nothing more than the strength of the tiger or wolf. Musashi realized this mistake at age 30 and diligently devoted himself to transcending it. Even at that, it took him until age 50. Perhaps not many people could go beyond the limits of techniques.

In his early days, Musashi was continually faced with win and loss, life and death. For him to live meant death for an opponent; for his opponent to win meant defeat for him. That world was the animal world of survival of the fittest. His sword could not go beyond *chikusho heiho* (animal/beastly tactics).

It is not strange to see sheep scatter at seeing a lion. This is an example of the animal instinct of self-preservation. Why Musashi stayed in the country and avoided Edo we may never know, but it may have been like the sheep's instinct to run from a lion. To criticize Musashi's whole lifetime, however, because of those he fought or did not fight while young does injustice to his recognition that those duels were won without an understanding of the secrets of swordsmanship.

I therefore cannot agree with the criticism of Musashi by the late Yamada Ittokusai Sensei. After the age of 50, Musashi truly experienced the Way of swordsmanship and truly attained Immovable Wisdom. We must not overlook that from that time forward, there was no particular way to train. He wrote that he spent his days and months distant and carefree. He had transcended the techniques of swordsmanship; swordsmanship as a means of "doing" something no longer remained. In this sense, swordsmanship itself becomes the purpose, the infinite dignity of man, the original principle, the Way. Beyond this there was nothing in particular to train for. There was no mountain peak for Musashi to reach; there was no path to follow. In other words, he was a retired man of the Way.

Such a state is called spending one's time leisurely. In Zen terminology: "In his advanced age of retirement, nothing happens; sound asleep in peace facing the blue mountain." He had entrusted his life to fate through the non-action of the play of *samadhi*. In the book *Homo Ludens* (Play of Man), Hunsinger describes the "play" of looking at blood (e.g. the art of bullfighting). If you can say that this is also true in the East, then it must be of this same state as the play of *samadhi*.

During his later years, Musashi was asked to create many works of painting and calligraphy. He also made sword guards and sculptures of the highest quality. He was able to master these many arts because "through the essence of swordsmanship, one should be accomplished in the arts and crafts." This is nothing but *myoyo*, the use of the wonderous, the miraculous, the creative, the creation of the Void. Musashi died at the age of 62 and was able therefore to taste and savor mastery of the mystery of the Way for no more than 10 years.

In Musashi's life, the art of killing leaped beyond death into *myoki*, wonderous "play."[5] This is not a state in which one can be removed from the idea of killing by mere thought. If that was true, the idea of giving life would be on the same level and could not be more than dualistic thought. The dualism of "killing" and "giving life" itself must both be killed and at the same time transcended. This in terms of the words of Harigaya Sekiun is *ainuke* (mutual passing). For all people and in all things one must be able to grasp this point, the state in which truth is fulfilled.

Why is this possible? Because man can negate negation. In terms of the *Hagakure* "The Way of the *samurai* is to die." In understanding this, man can attain self realization. According to Dogen Zenji, "Just forget and set free your mind and body and throw it into the house of the Buddha." One can negate oneself and, furthermore, one can also transcend that negation. *Hotoke no kata yori oko naware, kore ni shitagai mote yuku* (Whatever takes place should be in accord with the Buddha Mind and beyond the Buddha Mind).[6]

From the biological standpoint, there is no great difference between man and animals. But animals can only live as they were brought into this world by their mother. Man has an independent attribute: he can learn from experience and use it to alter the future. He is different from animals in that he has a creative characteristic, his reflective consciousness. One can live in a passive state like an animal, relying on the instinct of self-preservation, or, by negating the self and going beyond to the "Great Self," one can live his "True Self." This difference is obvious.

The Way of swordsmanship that Musashi attained at 50 went beyond the spirit of beastly fighting to the state of *ainuke* (mutual passing) described by Harigaya Sekiun. Here all the oppositions of Life and Death, Win and Lose, Strong and Weak are transcended by means of transcending the self. One can call it a Way to transcend Life and Death (all dualism). Is this achievement the same as Zen or is it different?

Se Mu I *(Giving fearlessness)*

Unlike the fame of Musashi, few people today have heard of Yamaoka Tesshu. As I have already written a book about Tesshu, I will try to avoid repetition in this discussion.

A person once asked Tesshu, "What is the secret of swordsmanship?" Tesshu answered, "It is entrusted to the Asakusa Kannon." The student at once went to Asakusa, searched everywhere in the temple and came to realize that the sign with the phrase "*Se Mu I*" (*Se*—give alms, carry out, conduct; *Mu*—void; *I*—fear) must be it. When he repeated this to Tesshu it is said that Tesshu answered "*Kekko*," (very good) and laughed.

Se Mu I comes from the sutra of the Bodhisattva of Great Compassion (Jpn. Kannon, Chin. Kwan Yin). In the sutra the Bodhisattva Kannon (Kanzeon Bosatsu Makasatsu) gives fearlessness in the midst of calamity of any kind. Consequently people call this bodhisattva *Se Mu I Sha*—the "Giver of Fearlessness."

The gift of fearlessness is the removal of fear or anxiety from the *kokoro* (mind, hearts) of people. To say it in another way, to give fearlessness is to give absolute peace of mind. If the highest stage of swordsmanship is to give fearlessness, then without doubt it is identical to Zen. Given this, the next question is what is the process by which a swordsman attains that state.

Here I would like to remind you of the quotation used at the beginning of this chapter from Nakae Toju's *Bun Bu Mondo*. He stated that there are those who do not revere Heaven's decree. They are atrocious, treacherous and have no respect for anything. They should either be brought to justice and punished, or a campaign should be launched against them so that the whole nation can be returned to peace. This is called *Bu* (Martial).

There are people who lack human qualities and whose behaviour is atrocious. They break the peace, violate the civil order and stand in the way of *Bundo* (*Bun*—civilization, literature, art, civil affairs; *Do*—Tao, Way). The *jitsuryoku* (force, ability, genuine strength) of *Budo* is needed to defeat and put down this trouble and disorder. In Zen it might be acceptable if priests do not have this force, but any Martial Way without *jitsuryoku* is not a genuine Martial Way.

Shimizu Jirocho once asked Tesshu, "Teacher, in an actual fight, swordsmanship is of no use, is it not?" Tesshu asked him to explain what he meant. Jirocho replied, "When I draw my sword and face the opponent, although I will probably get wounded, I simply glare and say *kono yaro* (you bastard!) and they usually run away." Tesshu then said "Is that so? Then with your long sword try to strike me. I will take you on with this short wooden sword and if you can even scratch me you will be the victor." Jirocho glared at Tesshu who was sitting cross-legged on the floor. After a moment Jirocho said to himself, "This is no good. No matter how I try, I cannot attack the teacher, I have no strength in my hands and feet. Teacher! I don't understand what is happening." Tesshu answered "This is the same as when you say *kono yaro* and your opponent is carried off his feet."

Tesshu then wrote the characters *Gan Fu Ho Ko Ki Hi Dai Jo Bu* and gave the paper to Jirocho. The phrase means it will not be fearlessness if your *gan* (glare, stare) does not have *koki* (vibrant force or dazzling light). Even without this force, you might argue that this frame of mind is equivalent to Zen, but it does not qualify as part of the Martial Ways.

For example, one can speak ill of the young Musashi and call his swordsmanship beastly. As you recall, in fighting for his life he sought victory with all of his strength and will. We recognize that this was an animal form of egotism and that by definition it is fundamentally opposite to Zen because Zen negates the ego. Zen works at a deeper level than the ego. But once that egotism is penetrated, the result is far more genuine than that achieved by seeking for No-self, No-Mind in mere abstractions.

As with Musashi, egotism can cut through egotism and thereby transcend it. There is then a synchronous change of "self," *sonomama* (just as is), to "No-Self." It is like the puckery persimmon that changes, *sonomama*, to a sweet persimmon. There is a firm and concrete nature to these things.

Suzuki Shozan in his work *Roankyo* puts it this way:

... present day instruction in zazen teaches to avoid awakening thoughts. But if you ask me, the thought of avoiding thoughts is already a thought. It's just that they have not realized this. To awaken great thoughts means that all small thoughts cannot be present. People today think that zazen is to be practiced without awakening thoughts and I am opposed to this. I awaken thoughts as great as Mt. Sumeru.

There are many teachers of Zen that teach that the world of Mu is like the empty sky. This will cause the immature Zen student to understand Void as something empty and this abstraction will lead to a flimsy enlightenment.

When one forgets his biological origins and characteristics, he separates himself from the multi-faceted nature of human existence. Such are the peace activists who call for "Peace!" in their hollow and feeble way. The current reality for all humans is truly severe: eat or be eaten. In the face of these conditions, it is time to unfold the great lessons of these teachings from *Budo*.

By putting our whole being into following the Way, the inevitable destruction of *aiuchi* (mutual killing and mutual striking) is transcended and becomes *ainuke* (mutual passing), the true swordsmanship stage of *Se Mu I*. Having first made that experience our own, it is our duty to share it with the world. Starting from the defensive posture of *aiuchi* (mutual killing and mutual striking), let our opponents cut the flesh that embraces nuclear weapons and we in turn will cut their bones. In this way we will be able to live and they will also prosper.[7]

In my opinion, we must step forward into the world of Zen and Swordsmanship in Oneness, the state of *ainuke* that appears with the sword that "Gives Life."

CHAPTER 5

Practical Zen

Practical Zen contains selections from Omori Roshi's writings that present solutions to problems encountered in Zen training. These solutions are based on Omori Roshi's own training and his translation of Buddhist philosophy into practical application.

Zen Training[1]

In order to train in Zen, the form of *zazen* need not always be taken. As long as the essence is the same as that of *zazen*, you can do anything. Eastern cultural arts and martial arts all have the same essence as that of *zazen*. This is what is called *samadhi*. Although I do not know too much about the West, I am sure that *samadhi* exists there. If you can attain this *samadhi*, whatever method you use is good.

At my *dojo*, in addition to *zazen*, we do Zen while holding a brush or a bamboo sword. In reality, we are holding the brush and writing words, or we are practicing *Kendo* with the bamboo sword. There is, however, the Zen of sewing, theZen of cutting vegetables, the Zen of keeping accounts, the Zen of typing. It is all right to have all kinds of Zen. That is why I think that sitting in meditation is not an essential condition in Zen.

You may wonder then, "Why do Zen priests do *zazen*?" It is because in *samadhi*, there is *ji-zanmai* (*samadhi* limited to a particular field of activity) and *oo-zanmai* (the great *samadhi*). *Ji-zanmai* is the *samadhi* only when you are doing something. For example, you are cutting vegetables, and you forget about cutting and the hand that is cutting. This is *ji-zanmai*. It can be achieved through your work or in the performing arts.

Oo-zanmai, however, is the fundamental and best *samadhi* that is universal and can be experienced during *zazen*. In an instant, the mind, body and breath become one, creating stability and *samadhi*. This *samadhi* can be used for anything and under any circumstances.

For example, a person who practices *Kendo* holds his bamboo sword and faces his opponent. If he forgets his opponent and his ego, enters *samadhi*, and truly experiences this state, then even when he puts his bamboo sword down, he must be able to maintain this frame of mind. Usually, however, it is a different world when he puts his bamboo sword down. A teacher of flower arrangement must also enter *samadhi* and become one with the flowers or she will not be able to make an arrangement that will move or touch people. But when she puts the scissors down, she reverts to her ordinary self.

People of ancient times have said the same thing. For instance, there is Suzuki Shozan (1579-1655) who was a *samurai* to the Tokugawas. Later, he became a Buddhist priest. His words have been collected in the book, *Roankyo*.[2] For example:

A certain person asked what the state of samadhi was. Shozan unsheathed his sword and held it in the seigan no kamae (the middle position) and said, "Well, do you understand? If you understand this, it is the easiest way for a samurai to achieve samadhi. That is so, but why can't the samurai understand Zen? Because when they lay their swords down, the state of samadhi is lost."

That is what he taught. In *ji-samadhi* you become skilled at becoming one with something, but even if you separate from that thing, you must maintain the state or be able to attain this state instantly. To say it in another way, when you do *zazen*, you attain *samadhi* during the thirty minutes to an hour that the incense is burning, but when you stand up, you return to your former state. This is not good.

The person who brought *zazen* from India to China was Bodhidharma.[3] In his teaching of *zazen*, many Indian traces still remain. It is said that the distinctive characteristic of Bodhidharma's *zazen* is *hekikan gyoju*. *Hekikan* means to face the wall and to see your true nature. It does not mean that you must always face a tangible wall. Your mind must become like a very steep wall that does not allow anything to approach. That is the state of *hekikan*. The meaning of *gyoju* is to concentrate your mind. In order to achieve *hekikan gyoju*, the monks in India meditated in the cool of the night under the moon and in a refreshing breeze. Sitting on rocks under trees, the monks would concentrate their minds and try to see their true natures.

From India *zazen* went to China and blended with the active and realistic national character of the Han race. From its original emphasis on serenity, Zen became dynamic. As a result, six generations after Bodhidharma, during Eno's (Hui-neng) time,[4] the foundation of Chinese Zen was established.

Eno defined *zazen* as, *za* (sitting) means "outwardly and under all circumstances, not to activate thoughts," and *zen* (meditation) is "internally to see the original nature and not become confused."[5]

That is why *zazen* does not only mean to sit with your legs folded. Being unaffected by your environment, with your true nature undisturbed, you go, remain still, sit and sleep. Going, remaining still, sitting and sleeping must all be *zazen*. Eno emphasized that *zazen* is not something that occurs only when sitting in a prescribed position.

Eno also said, "In this teaching of mine, from ancient times up to the present, all have set up no-thought as the main doctrine, no-form as the substance, and non-abiding as the basis."[6] The explanation of this is: "No-thought is not to think even when involved in thought. No-form is to be separated from form even when associated with form." When a thought occurs, leave it alone. Not becoming attached to the thought is no-thought. Even if you see shape or form, you must not hang on to it. If you see its *a priori* nature correctly, that is no-form. Non-attachment is not attaching to one thing or to one place but to keep flowing smoothly like water. This is the original nature of man.

The main point of Eno's teaching is to read the characters *"kensho"* not as to see (*ken*) your true self (*sho*) but as seeing is your true self. The action of seeing is the True Self. In other words, Buddha-nature equals the action of seeing. That is his view. The teaching of India is that in order to see one's True Self, one must watch one's Mind while quietly sitting on a rock under a tree. Eno, however, tells us, "The core of activities — for example, the activity of seeing, the activity of hearing, the activity of tasting, and so on (the activity of the five senses) — is True Nature. Eno is saying, "Seeing is your True Self." This is the unique expression of the philosophy of Chinese Zen. What Buddha and Bodhidharma experienced is exactly the same thing. This is the foundation of Chinese Zen. The Zen that has been handed down to Japan is an expression of Zen originally expressed by Eno. This expression underwent various changes. Upon reaching Rinzai (d. 866), for the first time, it took on the distinctive form of our Rinzai Zen. It can be said that Rinzai constructed a strong house on the foundation that Eno built.

In Eno's case, even if the action of seeing or the action of hearing is discussed, and what we call the body and mind are not separated, there is a tendency to give priority to the mind. Rinzai, however, asserts "the True Man without Rank" and expounds the body. Having no rank, not belonging to anything, and being free, this is the True Man. Of course, what he is referring to is the complete human being endowed with a body. Rinzai clearly stated that the basic principle of the philosophy of Zen is the activity of the mind-body, of the true and complete human being that is YOU—the person who is listening to my lecture—the True Man without Rank.

One could say that Rinzai's view of Zen is extreme, but the process of this development is quite important. Under Gunin (Hung-jen),[7] Chinese Zen separated into a northern and a southern branch. Jinshu's (Shen-hsiu)[8] line was named the Hokuzen (northern-gradual) School. Eno's line was named the Nanton (southern-sudden) School. With one great push, Rinzai advanced the Zen that Eno started into the domain of the concrete actions of human beings. That became the foundation of Japanese Rinzai Zen.

If we were to express these historical developments succinctly, we could say that Indian teachings emphasized mental aspects. Chinese Zen, however, perhaps because of the national characteristics of the Han people, placed the emphasis on the body. This form of Zen entered Japan and the complete person, the oneness of mind and body, the real and concrete action, in other words, *Zen-ki* (Zen dynamics or activity) came to be emphasized.

Zazen

As even Suzuki Shozan has said, "*Zazen* without *kiai* is a waste of time." Even if you do one hour of *zazen*, it is only one twenty-fourth of the day. During that sitting, incense is burned and you sit still without *kiai* for what is just an instant. That kind of *zazen* is useless. Everything that you do in your daily life must be *zazen*. This is the "non-sitting" form of *zazen*. Shido Bunan Zenji (1603–1676) also stressed this non-sitting *zazen*. If you understand this kind of *zazen*, you have almost accomplished your *zazen* training.

Zazen does not occur only during the time you cross your legs, fold your hands, regulate your breath, and concentrate on your *koan*. Walking on the street, reading a book, working in the kitchen, writing a letter, are all *zazen*. In any situation if you throw your entire self into what you are doing at that time, you will go into *samadhi*. That is what non-sitting *zazen* is. If you think that *zazen* is only meditating at a fixed time in a fixed posture, your *zazen* will not progress.

It has been customary from ancient times to begin one's *koan* training with the *koan Mu*. In trying to concentrate on *Mu*, if you buzz like a mosquito and say, "*Mu, mu,*" from the tip of your nose, you are wasting your time. If you don't say, "*MU!*" in one breath as if you are severing your life in *hisshi zanmai* (life or death *samadhi*), you will not be able to attain *satori*.

There is a man named Nakazawa who is a student of mine from the days at my Jikishin Dojo. He accomplished his realization by counting his breaths. When he counted "*Hitoo...tsu* (Japanese for one)," he entered *samadhi*. When he said,

"*Futaaaa...tsu*, (two)" he became "*Futaaaa...tsu*." In this way, he attained the absolute present and was enlightened. You can become enlightened splendidly by counting breaths. It is better to do it that way than to say "*Mu*" only with the tip of your nose.

When you are doing *zazen*, you must exhale thoroughly. If you do that seriously and with all your being, anyone can realize their True Self.

Zenjyo - the Kiai of Zazen[9]

When Suzuki Shozan was asked what the *kiai* of *samadhi* was, he unsheathed his long sword, took a *Kendo* stance, and said, "It is this. You must not lose this *kiai*." "Not losing this *kiai*" does not mean being ceremonious and pretentious, nor does it mean being physically unyielding. Hakuin Zenji said that the continuation of correct consciousness does not mean that we should become like the string holding the beads of the *juzu* (Buddhist rosary), rather we must become the beads.

This is an important point. We must put our entire being into each thing that we are doing. When we are writing, we must throw our bodies and minds into each letter and enter *samadhi*. When we are doing *zazen*, we must become *zazen* and be in *samadhi* moment by moment. In this way, although we are tense and strained when we start to train, later we must gradually become soft and pliant. When we become soft and refined, our inner being becomes full of vital energy. This is real perfection.

To reach this condition, we must regulate our breath. Regulating the breath is not losing *kiryoku* (vital energy) of the *tanden*. It is said that the *tanden* is so many inches from the navel, but it is not located in any fixed place. Everyone is different; therefore, we cannot say that the *tanden* is located two inches below the navel. The *tanden* is the center point which balances the entire body. It is not one definite point on the body. Each person must find it for herself or himself. When we breath out, we must use the lower abdomen. When we inhale, we loosen our muscles, and new air will fill our lungs. If we do this, oxygen will unite with red blood cells and circulate through the whole body. This becomes the basis for *kiryoku*. As we breath out all the air we can, all strength will leave the shoulders and the strength of the *tanden* will soften the abdomen and make the energy sink to the *tanden*.

When we can breathe out no more and relax our muscles, in an instant air will fill the lungs. Then we breathe out again. Like the piston of a bellows heating up coal, this heats up the energy in our bodies. Our lower back will set its posture naturally, and our spines will straighten. We stand correctly because the *kiryoku* within us becomes complete. Fatigue is overcome, and we become revitalized. This is a concrete way to regulate and perfect *kiryoku*.

In this way we are able to walk on the Way with little effort. We do not have to act superior. We need not be ashamed no matter where we go even if we go before God or Buddha. We are not ashamed of any part of ourselves.

By breathing in the manner mentioned above, we cultivate our *kiryoku*. Furthermore, by our actions we make moral *kiryoku* flourish also. With our minds and bodies, we will be full of vigor. To perfect *kiryoku* does not mean to throw out our chests, it means to be composed and dignified. We must have an awe-inspiring *kiryoku* which is disturbed by nothing.

This is what is called *zazen*. This is what is called Nio Zen.[10]

Koan and Realization in Zen[11]

Basically the word *"koan"* refers to the instances in which ancient Zen masters were enlightened by some word or action. Originally it came from *Kofu no Antoku* which was an official edict of ancient China that absolutely had to be obeyed once it had been proclaimed. In Zen the term *koan* refers to cases which contain principles that a student of Zen has to realize absolutely.

In the beginning of Zen in China the teacher did not give the student a specific question to work on. Each student tackled a problem himself and looked to his teacher to guide him in solving it. For example, take the incident between Bodhidharma and Eka[12] who later carried on Bodhidharma's line in China:

[Eka said,] "Your disciple's mind is not yet pacified. I beg you, my teacher, please pacify my mind."

Bodhidharma said, "Bring the mind to me, and I will pacify it."

Eka said, "I have searched for the mind these many years and am still unable to get hold of it."

Bodhidharma said, "There! It is pacified once and for all."[13]

During the period after Eka and before the systematization of Koan Zen in the 9th century, the following story illustrates the nature of the interactions between master and student.[14]

When Nangaku Ejo (Nan-yueh Hai-jang)[15] *went to see the 6th patriarch Eno, Eno faced him and said, "Where did you come from?"*

Nangaku answered, "I came from Mt. Tung-shan."

Eno responded, "What walked here?"

Nangaku Ejo could not say that his feet did the walking, nor could he say that his body had walked there. All he could do was to try to enlighten himself by concentrating on "what had walked there." This is the form that the *koan* took in the beginning. As Zen masters repeatedly gave such cases to students to work on, the cases gradually became systematized.

Usually, you *kufu* (to strive or wrestle with, to try to find the way out) a *koan* through *zazen*, but you can also concentrate on the *koan* while you are involved in some activity: What is this that is now working? Who is this that is drinking tea? Who is this that is talking? If you are always searching in this way, you have achieved a way of training.

Practical Zen 123

Over time questions, such as "What is Buddha? What is the meaning of Bodhidharma coming from India?" which spontaneously arose were systematized into a fixed format from the latter part of the Tang dynasty in the last half of the 9th century till the Sung dynasty in the 13th century. But it was not until works such as the *Hekigan Roku* were published that the system that we know today became established. This work is divided into one hundred cases, and about one hundred forty personnages appear in them. Master Engo Kokugon (Yuan-wu Ko-ch'in)[16] commented on the main point of each case.

During the Sung Dynasty Master Daie Soko (Ta-hui Tsung-kao)[17] encountered the following problem. He thought, "These days the students doing *sanzen* (private interview with the master in which the student presents his answer to the *koan*) say things that are too good. For beginners, they do too well. Perhaps they have a text." He discovered that students had memorized the *Hekigan Roku* word for word and were using it in their answers. Master Daie said that this would not help them, and it is said that he collected all the copies of *Hekigan Roku* and burned them.

In the present day *koan* system, a first *koan* we almost always give to the beginner is, "Does a dog have Buddha nature?" This is the *koan* of Master Joshu (Chao-chou)[18] who lived during the Tang dynasty in China. He explained Zen in everyday terms. In the history of Zen I think he was one of the greatest masters. A priest asked Joshu, "Does a dog have Buddha nature?" Joshu said, "*Mu*." That became a *koan*. What exactly is this *Mu*?

This is the first *koan* in the *Mumonkan*.[19] The editor of this book, Mumon Ekai (Wu-men Hui-k'ai),[20] gave some advice on how to *kufu* this *koan*:

Don't you want to pass the barrier? Then throw yourself into this "Mu," with your 360 bones and 84,000 pores, making your whole body one great inquiry. Day and night work intently at it. Do not attempt nihilistic or dualistic interpretations. The search for an answer is like having swallowed a red hot iron ball. You try to vomit it but cannot.

Cast away your illusory discriminating knowledge and consciousness accumulated up to now, and keep working harder. After a while, when your efforts come to fruition, all the oppositions (such as in and out) will naturally be identified. You will then be like a dumb person who has had a wonderful dream: he only knows it personally, within himself. Suddenly you break through the barrier; you will astonish heaven and shake the earth.[21]

In short, Master Mumon is teaching us to question where our mind works and to look for the source by ourselves. Where does this *Mu* come from? We must concentrate completely on *Mu*. Not only must we become one with *Mu*, we must transcend it. How do we achieve this?

Mumon uses the expression, "360 bones and 84,000 pores," which, during his time, meant the entire human body. In other words, he explains that we must become *Mu* by using our whole body and all our energy. We must concentrate everything on *Mu*.

If you do that, you will be able to experience the same *samadhi* as the Buddha did after he abandoned his severe physical training and did *zazen*. Shakyamuni thought that inflicting severe pain on the body would free the spirit. In the end he realized that the mind and body were one. He realized that he could not be liberated by punishing his body. He abandoned harsh physical training, went to the foot of the Himalayas, and did *zazen*. He was constantly in the state of "Absolute *Mu*." At sunrise he saw the morning star and realized, "It is not that there is nothing. There is this form here that I call myself looking at the morning star. Moreover, this form is not only a simple 'self;' it is a point that is the center of an infinite circle; it is the center of the entire Universe." When you are in absolute *samadhi* and a stimulus breaks this state, suddenly such a realization will occur. That is enlightenment.

Though this *koan Mu* had been used since ancient times, about 250 years ago Hakuin Zenji felt that it should not become over used and began to use the *koan*, "What is the sound of one hand clapping?" This *koan* became very popular because it creates doubt easily.

If you hit both hands together, a sound will be produced. But what is the sound of one hand clapping? It is what we must call the absolute sound. This sound must be uncovered. Then you will realize the Original Nature, the eternal life which is not merely the life before you were born but the perpetual life that exists before the birth of your parents. We call it the True Self.

The first question that comes to mind in relation to Hakuin's *koan* is "Does one hand make a sound?" The next question is "What could it be?" It is said that the method of solving a *koan* is to become a mass of doubt. This absolute query is, at the same time, the absolute solution. To put it another way, when the doubter and the *koan* are in opposition, the two do not become a single mass of doubt. Instead of making the *koan* an object and examining it analytically, we must concentrate on becoming one with it. In other words, the person who is doubting and the object of the doubt unite and become one mass of doubt. Becoming the mass of doubt is the method of solving the *koan*, and breaking through this mass of doubt is enlightenment.

The Zen method is to totally negate all accepted facts and dualities and then to re-affirm them.[22] *Sanzen* is indispensible for training with *koan*. In this method the Zen master who has already passed through the *koan* and the more experienced senior students lead the less experienced junior students. But rather than giving hints, when presented with an answer, the Zen master must thoroughly negate it, saying that everything is wrong, and must drive the student into the realm of Absolute *Mu*.

The student must be trapped like a mouse that has gone into a bamboo cylinder — he cannot advance forward because of the bamboo joint, yet he cannot go back. The Zen master's job is to push his student into that kind of state. With his dualistic thinking driven into a corner, the student will be transformed and led to the realm of absolute freedom.

In the monastery, everything is well thought out. During *sanzen*, the *jikijitsu* (head monk) pulls out the beginners who are sitting in the *zazen* hall. He forces them to go to see their teacher in *sanzen*. The Zen master and the head monk work together to drive the student into a corner. For example, there was a Zen master named Mamiya Eiju. When he was a monk at Tenryu-ji, in *sanzen* Master Gassan hit him with his *shippei* (stick carried by the master). When he went back to the meditation hall, the head monk scolded him, "What are you doing! Go back again!" In the end, unable to tolerate it any longer, Mamiya retreated to the bathroom. It is said that he hid there for one whole night. This kind of earnest person quickly reaches his limit.

If one is not serious and does not reach one's limit, the experience will be late and shallow. Whether asleep or awake, we must *kufu* our *koan* without pause and become a mass of doubt. Then because of some stimulus, we are able to break through that state and we have a realization. That is what enlightenment is.

How to Work on the Koan

Omori Roshi was once asked about a method for solving *koan*, "Roshi, in the first chapter of the *Mumonkan*, it is written, 'Twenty-fours hours a day, you must always *kufu Mu* and try to find an answer.' But some people say, 'Put all of your energy into what you are doing at the moment.' Which is the right way?" Roshi replied:

> When you are working on your first *koan*, just as it is written in the *Mumonkan*, you should *kufu* this *koan* twenty-four hours a day whether you are awake or asleep. As you gradually advance

in your *koan* training, however, you should put all of your energy into what you are doing at the moment. Concentrate on your *koan* when you are doing *zazen*. But for a lay person who has a job, even if it is his first *koan*, it is different from a monk whose sole job is to meditate. When the lay person is working, he should put everything into working. If he has even a moment of spare time, then, he should return to his *koan*. However, during a *sesshin*, it would be ideal if one could be in the state of *koan samadhi* while searching for an answer to the *koan*.

When Shido Bunan Zenji received his *koan*, "From the beginning nothing exists," from Gudo Toshoku Zenji, he was always seeking the answer. One day when he was making a rope, he became absorbed in his *koan*. He forgot the hand that was twisting the rope and could not twist anymore. Gudo Zenji was watching on the side and said to those who were near him, "If you can concentrate this much on your *koan*, there is no doubt that you can have a realization." That is how to get an answer to your first *koan*.

How to Read the Sutra[23]

When I was a youth, I once went to Lake Towada in Akita Prefecture. Close to this lake are the ruins of the place where a priest named Nansobo had trained. According to the guide's explanation, Nansobo wore iron *geta* (Japanese sandals) and travelled all over Japan. He decided that the place where the cloth thongs of his *geta* broke would be where he would train for the rest of his life. When he got to Lake Towada, the thongs suddenly broke and he resolved that this would be his life-long place of training. A huge snake had been living there before him and refused to let him take his home away so they began battling. Suddenly Nansobo began to recite the Lotus *Sutra*. Each word of the Lotus *Sutra* became an arrow and pierced the body of the snake. Bleeding and writhing, the snake slithered away.

Whether true or not, the story relates that when Nansobo recited the *sutra*, each word became a piercing arrow. I think that this is a wonderful way to read the *sutra*. If you cannot do it that way, you cannot say that you read the *sutra*. The meaning of the *sutra* does not matter. If you want to study the *sutra*, you should put the *sutra* on a desk in a quiet place and leisurely read it while savoring it. Then you will interpret the words and be able to understand the meaning. That is the scholarly way of reading it.

Do not concern yourself with that. If you are going to read the *sutra* for your training, you must read the *sutra* like Nansobo and make each word an arrow that pierces. If we were to express this in Zen terminology, we would say, *"Tekisui Tekito"* (Each drop of water, each drop of ice). If you don't read the *sutra* as if you have become each drop (that is, without becoming each word moment by moment), the *sutra* will not have any effect. Straighten your back, push your energy down to the *tanden*, and with your eyes fixed, read the *sutra*. Read as much as you can in one breath. Mind and body becoming one, you enter *samadhi*. It is possible to be liberated by reading *sutra*.

If you are merely reading it with the tip of your nose, even if you say, *"Makahanya…,"* it will be useless. It is easy for us to concentrate our attention while reading aloud. When you are reading with many people, you must read as though your neighbor's voice is going into your ears and out of your mouth. If you don't do that, the recitation will be scattered and not unified.

Keep your breath long and breathe out as long as you can. Then it will be easy to collect your energy. If you cannot get your energy together, even if the *sutra* is short, do it over and over again.

If you read the *sutra* in this way, you can experience mind and body as *ichinyo* (Oneness: one and separate at the same time). You do not have to read aloud. In fact, it is more difficult to read the *sutra* silently than aloud. It is easier to unify mind and body by reading aloud. To unify the mind and body by reading silently requires training in daily life. In this way, you can cultivate the ability to enter *samadhi*. The body will automatically become erect.

I have this anecdote about the *sutra*. After the war I became a priest and went to the Toyama home to recite the *sutra* on the anniversary of Ryusuke Sensei's death. A person wearing baggy work pants entered the room through the garden. He placed a huge book of *sutra* on the small table in front of the Buddhist altar. He recited a *sutra* in a very deep voice that was like billowy clouds arising from the bottom of a very deep cavern. In the middle of the recitation, there were sometimes pauses which were quite long. I think that he was probably in *samadhi*. In a little while, he would start to recite again in the same voice. Sitting in the back, I was totally astonished. I was too embarassed to read the *sutra* after such a recitation and went home after I had offered incense without reading the *sutra*.

This man was Hamachi Hachiro, a lawyer and the father of Toyama Ryusuke's wife. He was a believer of the Diamond *Sutra* and had been enlightened through this *sutra*. Having done *sanzen* in the Soto sect, he had received the name, Layman Tensho. (Once when he was critically ill and unconscious, he continued to chant the *sutra*. It was so ingrained in him.)

Continuation of Correct and True Consciousness[24]

According to Hakuin Zenji, "*Shonen Sozoku*" (Continuation of correct and true consciousness) is not like the thread that holds the rosary beads together but is like the beads themselves. He is saying that consciousness must become each one of the beads. If moment by moment we are completely concentrated in the present, our consciousness will be discontinuously continuous, and we will be able to go right through. Hakuin's words are those of a person who has had a personal experience. If a person who has not had such an experience says "*Shonen Sozoku*," he will think that it means to continue to possess right thought. That is impossible. Rather it means to become what you are doing at the moment. When we practice *Hitsuzendo* (attaining the Way through a brush), what is the feeling with which we write a line? The line is a continuum of the discontinuous. We are not merely writing a line; we are putting our entire life into each dot. Many unconnected dots come together to form a line. In other words, we are practicing "*Shonen Sozoku*" with a brush. Being attentive to everything, we strike each dot completely. We write with the feeling that each dot continues and forms a line. We are not merely drawing a line.

At the moment when we perfectly experience the Absolute Now in our daily lives, the discontinuous continues. For the first time, all our activities come alive. For example, even entertainers must have this. Even before the curtain rises and he makes his entrance, an actor in a play must already BE his part. He does not suddenly become his part when the curtain rises. Even when he leaves the stage and goes from the wings to his dressing room, he must maintain the same presence as he did on stage. If he does not do this, his presence will not linger on the stage. But if he does not relax and goes to the dressing room with the same feeling that he had while he was on stage, that atmosphere will continue on the stage. The feeling will linger with the audience. That kind of mental phenomenon exists. Zeami (founder of the Noh theater) calls this "the Doing-Nothing-Time" in his book the *Flower Mirror*. If you are not careful about this "Doing-Nothing-Time," the before and after of one's acting will not come alive.

If you only feel fulfilled when you are doing something, what will happen at other times? It means that during the 24 hours of a day, you are only really alive for two or three hours when you throw yourself into activity. On the other hand, if you feel fulfilled even if you are not doing anything, you will be fulfilled all the time. That is the training that we do during *Hitsuzendo*. In that way, we draw each dot completely. Those dots continue discontinuously and form a line. That is our training; it is a way of life.[25]

How to Train While Engaging in Work

Studying oneself is one's great work in life. It is a fundamental necessity. If a person seriously considers it, however, he should quit his job, and, just as Buddha and other well-known priests of old did, train intently. It is also what I should have done, but since I had no intention to do so, I had to train while engaged in work. Presently most of the people who have devoted themselves to Zen training are people who are working in society. In that case, they should make time to sit in the morning and evening. They should go to Zen groups where they will be encouraged to try harder or broaden their spiritual knowledge. I think that these are the normal means available to lay people.

While I was a lay person, I was told that I should meditate for four hours a day. That was not an easy thing. Because of the nature of my job, I had more free time than most people, but I also had my students to take care of and my wife and children to support. It was almost impossible to devote four hours a day to meditation. Though I tried my best, I could only manage three hours a day. For those who have their own business, even three hours must be difficult.

I think that for those who are busy with many activities, it is necessary even for their health to get up a little earlier and to go to sleep a little later and do thirty minutes of *zazen* morning and evening. I must say that those who cannot even sit for thirty minutes morning and evening do not have the necessary desire to do *zazen*. Those who have a serious desire will abandon everything and earnestly sit for two hours a day. In addition, utilizing even short intervals—while driving a car or riding in a train, while walking, or while waiting for someone—they will regulate their breathing, put their strength into their *tanden*, tighten their anus, and concentrate on their *koan*. Those who do this will develop great strength.

When you work, you must throw your entire mind and body into your work. Dogen Zenji said, "Throw your entire mind and body into Buddha's house." You must throw your body and mind into your work. When you deal with another person, you must become one with that person. When you read a book, you must go into the book. That is what it means. You must become one with whatever you are doing. In the monastery, there is *samu* (training with work): cultivating the vegetable garden, cleaning the garden, and so on. By (throwing yourself entirely into *samu* and) entering *samadhi*, you can lose yourself and conquer delusion.

If you think of your work as *samu*, there is no other way to train but to work intently and enter working *samadhi* completely. Usually people think that sitting is *munen muso* (no thought) or *kuku jaku jaku* (the state of quiet emptiness) and thus meant to feel nice and peaceful. They think that *zazen* is the easy way to enter the *Dharma* Gate, but they are making a big mistake. Suzuki Shozan has said, "If you are going to do *zazen* with no *kiai*, it would be far better to sing *utai* (a Noh drama text) with vigor." Further, Hakuin Zenji has said, "If it is the kind of *zazen* in which you say, '*Munen muso*,' and enter *kuku jaku jaku* and feel good, it would be better to gamble with all your might."

In this way concentrating on your work with a courageous mind is called "working *zazen*." There is, however, one thing which you must not forget. If one of these three things—great faith, great doubt, or great determination—is missing, you cannot complete your training. Great faith is unwaveringly to have the conviction that from the beginning we are Buddha. Great doubt is your mind and body becoming a mass of doubt; your entire body and spirit becomes the *koan* or counting. Great determination is the resolution, "Damn it! I will see this to the end!" You must possess all three. Not one may be missing. If you possess all three, no matter how you train, you will be able to achieve a great and total enlightenment and be able to accomplish the *Dharma*.

Satori[26]

If you think that giving the answer to a *koan* is *satori* (enlightenment), you are very much mistaken. The answer to a *koan* is not difficult. If you have a little intelligence, you can give many answers. If that is what you call *satori*, you don't have to undergo painful training. To train with all your might and with suffering is to physically experience absolute emptiness. One must train fervently and intently. *Satori* is to know your True Self. Truly knowing yourself and realizing it, you will have to show it in every action. Then the training that you do after *satori* will be carried out thoroughly. It takes a long time to get there.

Zen is not merely entering *zazen samadhi* and sitting like a frog. In the end, it is what is called *jyoe enmyo*. *Jyo* is the *samadhi* that emerges from *e*, *prajna*-wisdom (transcendental, intuitive wisdom). The development of *prajna*-wisdom is the goal of Zen. *Enmyo* means that *samadhi* and *prajna*-wisdom are not different. If you develop *prajna*-wisdom, you will be able to see things correctly. What is called *shoken* (correct and true seeing) will emerge. Even in the *Rinzai Roku*,[27] *shinsho no kenge* (correct and true seeing) is frequently stressed.

The attainment of correct and true seeing is the objective of Zen. With this kind of correct insight, we will be able to make decisions and choices. Without it, it is easy to confuse the correct and incorrect. Especially during these turbulent times, we must be able to see clearly the realities of our environments, our societies, our civilizations. That is our duty.

Training after Realization[28]

In Zen there is a *koan* called *Hokyo Zammai* (*Samadhi* as a Reflection from the Precious Mirror). It is a *koan* of a very high degree. A mirror reflects objects. If an object appears, it reflects it. We must become like a mirror. That is *Hokyo Zammai*. When I passed this *koan*, the Zen master guided me for three years to use this concretely as my training in my daily life. In this way, I was able to experience first hand the Buddhist doctrine I had understood through *koan* training.

There is a *koan* called "*sho hen ego zanmai,*" *sho* becomes *hen* and *hen* becomes *sho*. *Sho* is sameness, and *hen* is the aspect of difference. *Sho* and *hen* alternating freely is the state of *sho hen ego zanmai*, the blending of sameness and difference. It is not enough to just understand this theoretically. It is said that one must train and experience it for three years. If you train in it for three years, when you meet something, you will just naturally reflect it. In order to really know that what is reflected is really you, you must train in your daily life. If you do this, you will experience first hand that all things are one. I think that is what is called "training after realization."

Even if you know *sho* and *hen* in theory, your knowledge will be abstract and useless. But if you train in daily life, even if you cannot attain it perfectly, you will be able to come close. Here we can say that Buddhist wisdom becomes Buddhist compassion or that from this wisdom, compassion arises. Through actual practice, action emerging from the oneness of wisdom-compassion can be realized. If this cannot be done, a universal great compassion will not spontaneously come forth.

If you have a realization, you should make a one hundred eighty degree change. Even after realization, however, life itself is the continuation of one's training. The theories that you have realized through realization must influence your daily life and your character. Striving to do this kind of after realization training is the principle of training.

How to Train[29]

There are two ways to train. One is to train through studying the theories of Buddhist doctrine. This is called "Entrance by Reason." The other way is to actually experience these theories which is "Entrance by Conduct."

Entering by Reason, one realizes that all existence is like a dream, like an illusion, like foam, like dew, or like thunder. Existence has no concrete form. In Buddhism, we speak of Void and Emptiness, but that is not to say that there is nothing. In Buddhism, all things that exist are living by cause and condition. This is the causal standpoint that is taken.

Buddha renounced the world in which he lived at the age of 29, and at 35 he attained enlightenment. He realized his True Self. From ancient times it is said that in the Garland *Sutra*, for the first time, he related the substance of his experience to his five friends who had previously forsaken him. The Garland *Sutra* explains the materialization of existence from the standpoint of the passage of time. From the spatial standpoint of the materialization of existence, the doctrine of reality of the Tendai Sect explains the substance of this existence. Where the doctrine of cause and condition of the Garland *Sutra* crosses with the doctrine of reality of the Tendai Sect and where the attribute of time crosses with the attribute of space is where all existence is. If you clearly understand this theory of Buddhist philosophy, it is called Entrance by Reason.

Because of conditions, things change. Among the things that change depending on conditions, none has a concrete body. They are always changing. In this world nothing remains static even for a second. For example, even the floor and the walls are not fixed bodies. If there is such a thing as a fixed, unchanging body, why do things get old? Why do they gradually go bad? It is because all things possess an element of time.

Existence changes. If you leave something alone and it gets old, that means that it possesses the trait of time. The fact that it has the character of time means that it has no static substance. That is what we call Void or Emptiness. If you think that this means that nothing is there or that this means emptiness in the relative sense, that is contrary to what the Buddha realized. There are, however, many who train in Zen who think that Void or Emptiness means nothingness. That is proof that they have not done any studying. Without entering through Buddhist theory, without studying even a little, can you become enlightened just by sitting like a toad?

Such an idiotic thing cannot happen. There is no Buddhist law that is not supported by Buddhist theory. That is why entering by Reason must be made very clear. As I said before, this means realizing that nothing that exists is a static entity. Everything is always flowing and changing.

Entrance by Conduct means to physically experience Buddhist theory. How do we physically experience this? Our mind and body are the "mother body" that gives rise to 84,000 (infinite) earthly desires. Denouncing that body, we must pull out the 84,000 earthly desires one by one. That is what is called entering by Conduct.

After doing *zazen* and becoming enlightened, even though you have finished your formal training, there is still after enlightenment training. It is not correct to think that because you have been enlightened, everything is fine. After being enlightened and understanding Buddhist theory, is when your true training begins. It is said that you must train for your whole life.

Training cannot even be accomplished in one lifetime. One must train from rebirth to rebirth. Yamaoka Tesshu (1836-1888), a great swordsman, calligrapher, statesman, and Zen master, copied the *sutra* every evening. His younger brother said to him, "Even though you copy the *sutra* as you do, you will not be able to copy all of them in one lifetime, will you?"

Tesshu answered, "But I will continue to copy them. First I will write them all in the printed style. When that is finished, I will write them in the cursive style. When that is finished, I will write in the more flowing cursive style. I will be reborn many times into this human form to do it." Tesshu is saying that it does not matter if such a thing can be done. No matter what, it will be done. That was Tesshu's aspiration for his training.

That is what training is all about. Just having done a little *zazen* and thinking that you have trained will not amount to anything. After training, realizing your True Self, and completing all the *koan*, then your true training begins. If you do not do this, you will not know what training really is. Even I finished all the *koan* of the Tekisui school and received *inka* (formal approval to carry the Zen lineage from teacher to student). Then when I was told that I had graduated from Zen, I truly understood what training was. Because I had completed the course on *koan*, I was able to understand the *koan* system. I was able to get a view from the top. For the first time I realized what training was. From that point on, my real training began. That is what is called Entrance by Conduct. That is the training that continues from rebirth to rebirth to rebirth.

CHAPTER 6

Teisho:
The World of the Absolute Present

This chapter is a compilation of *teisho* given by Omori Sogen. A *teisho* is a talk given by the Zen master to express his understanding of the *Dharma* before the Buddha. Although metaphysical in content, these talks are not intended to be formal philosophical discourse.

Sanboin - The Three Truths of the Dharma

From ancient times it has been said that there are 84,000 doctrines in Buddhism. To lay bare their secrets or to capture on paper so many doctrines with one phrase is impossible.

Even in Zen, the masters say there are more than 1700 *koan* we must pass through to realize the True Self. Shakyamuni Buddha, the founder of Buddhism, however, when asked, "What is the *Dharma* principle?" replied "For 49 years I did not say a thing," and turned away. On the other hand, as if giving Maha Kasho the secret of Buddhism, Shakyamuni held up a flower and said, "I have the all-pervading True *Dharma*, incomparable *Nirvana*, exquisite teaching of formless form. It does not rely on letters and is transmitted outside scriptures. I now hand it to Maha Kasho."[1]

It has been said that Shakyamuni was irrational for saying such contradictory things, but indeed there is no other way to make people understand the *Dharma* principle. For 49 years exhausting all explanations, using many tens of thousands of words, Shakyamuni could not explain the *Dharma* principle. On the other hand, even one word is not necessary to explain the *Dharma* principle. The *Dharma* principle has two faces: 1) No matter how many words one uses, one cannot explain the principle. 2) No words are needed in explanation.

It is like drinking water. The person who drinks knows whether it is hot or cold. Unless a person realizes the *Dharma* principle through his own training, it has no meaning. At the same time from another perspective, it is also true that the power to persuade others of the [reality of the] *Dharma* principle is necessary. For this reason, in India, the logic of Buddhism was developed. If not saying a thing is true, then the 84,000 doctrines are also true. How shall we explain the *Dharma* principle even provisionally?

Without exception the things of this world can be considered from two perspectives: space-being and time-being. In the final analysis, the essence of a thing can be clarified from the perspective of time, looking at the stages of development, or from the perspective of space, looking at the reason for something being where it is. For example, through understanding the occurrence, change and development of phenomenon as progression in time, we can understand why phenomena exist as they are. On the other hand, from the perspective of space, we can analyze things into their elements, reconstitute them, and scientifically investigate their nature. Looking at phenomena through time is *engiron*, the doctrine of dependent origination (cause and conditions), and looking at phenomena through space is *jissoron*, the doctrine of the real state of all things. Even if this is said, in the actual world the temporal and spatial aspects of tangible objects cannot be separated. The relation between time and space is like that between water and waves. Time and space, like appearance and substance, are one thing. If we try to understand phenomenon intellectually or theoretically, however, there is no way to do this other than through the two perspectives described earlier. What is called knowledge is originally based on the judgment that there is time and space.

From this relative perspective, understanding the doctrines of Buddhism in terms of time is the first of the three truths: All phenomenal things are impermanent. To grasp the doctrines of Buddhism in terms of space is the second truth: Phenomenal things exist only by conditions; they have no substance in themselves. The third truth is: *Nirvana* is the state of tranquility. These three are the *sanboin*, the three truths of Buddhism. The three truths are definite and unchanging. They are the absolute truths of Buddhism. I think that any teachings that differ from this are heresy. The three truths are the standard which separate Buddhism from other teachings.

To understand being in terms of time is to see occurrence, change, and development (*engiron*). To see being in terms of space is to see the real state of all things (*jissoron*). But as I have said before, like water and waves, or substance and appearance, time and space cannot be considered as separate. For a moment, however, let us separate the two. Then we have the Hosso Sect (the Consciousness-only School), which follows Vasubandhu's teaching and stands on the principle of *engiron*. Vasubandhu's commentaries on the Avatamsaka *Sutra* were translated into Chinese. Based on them the Juji School was established. From this school the Kegon School (Chi Hua-yen) emerged. Accordingly the principle of the Kegon is *engiron*.

In contrast the Sanron Sect follows Nargajuna's teaching and stands on the principle of *jissoron*. Historically in China the philosophy of the Tendai Sect has a very deep relation to the Sanron Sect and belongs to the *jissoron* category. Emon (Hui-wen),[2] the monk who lived in the Northern and Southern Dynasty (420–589), was a famous scholar of the Sanron Sect (Chin. San-lun-tsung) and established the basis of the Tendai Sect (Chin. T'ien-t'ai). These, however, are just temporary separations and cannot be maintained in the strict, scholarly sense. Both these doctrines (*engiron* and *jissoron*) are like two strands intertwined to make a single rope.

If we overemphasize the temporal perspective of *engi*, we lean towards differentiation. If we overemphasize the spatial perspective, we lean towards non-differentiation, the equality of all things. At the meeting of time and space, at that point there is the absolute present, the Middle Way, the tranquility of *Nirvana*. The three truths are to be understood three dimensionally. [ed. note: Time is like a vertical axis, and space a horizontal axis. At the intersection of the two is *Nirvana*, but on a higher, third dimension.]

Shogyo Mujo - All Things are Impermanent

This is the first truth. *Gyo* refers to the Sanskrit term for *samsara*, meaning "all things." At the same time *gyo* means *adhva-samsara*, or "always changing." The first truth indicates that there is nothing which remains constant; everything is flowing and changing. Nothing is absolutely fixed.

Ordinarily we think that the world we come into contact with is a fixed reality. The world, however, is like the water of a river always flowing, never stopping for a moment. The ancient Greek philosopher Heraclitus said, "Everything changes." Everything has time in it, therefore everything changes.

Time is not something which exists independent of things; it is within things themselves. For example, if there is a pen here, it will gradually get older and be worn away. In the end it cannot be used. In Buddhism there are four kalpas, *jo* (creation), *ju* (existence), *e* (destruction), and *ku* (annihilation). Everything goes through this process of four stages because everything has time. Truly we can say that because everything flows and changes, everything has life. For example, if a single grain of rice or a small piece of meat is fixed and unchanging, human life cannot continue even for a day. The rice grain becomes cooked rice; it is digested and becomes liquid. The nutrients are then absorbed into and nourish the body. This is because the rice grain is not fixed but changing.

What causes this flowing and changing? In Buddhist terminology, it is said this world is *hokai* (the realm of reality). In this case *ho* means the law of cause and conditions. Cause becomes effect; effect becomes cause. [Depending on conditions, different effects emerge. For example a seed kept in a drawer will not bloom, but when planted and given water and fertilizer, it will bloom. In the final analysis, cause, conditions, and effects are one.] Reality changing according to the law of cause and conditions is *hokkai*.

This is what Shakyamuni Buddha referred to when he said, "He who sees *engi* (cause and conditions) clearly sees the *Dharma*." The law of cause and conditions means that beings are created and destroyed in accordance with cause and conditions. Nothing in this world exists by itself. Everything is interdependent. If you view this world from the perspective of time, everything changes continuously depending on cause and conditions. People commonly mistake the theory of Buddhism as cause and effect, but the theory of Buddhism is based on cause and conditions.

Let us imagine that we have a radish seed. In this seed is the cause for a big, two foot long radish root. The theory of cause and effect ties cause and effect directly together and concludes that this seed will inevitably become a two foot long radish. In Buddhism this is not so. We recognize that the seed has the potential to become a radish, but the seed must be planted in the field, given fertilizer, water, and sunlight. In addition the field must be weeded. Under these conditions, the radish, which is the effect, will grow. Depending on the conditions, however, a big, long radish or an inedible radish may result. The effect is something uncertain and depends on conditions.

Everything is cause, conditions, and effect; limitless differentiations are born from the movement of cause and conditions. In the Agama *Sutra* it is said, "All things appear and disappear because of the concurrence of causes and conditions. Nothing ever exists entirely alone; everything exists in relation to everything else." This *sutra* illustrates the mutual interdependence of everything.

In the theory of cause and conditions, there are four phases: *gokan-engi, arayashiki-engi, shinnyo-engi,* and *hokkai-engi.*[3]

Hokkai-engi is the final theory. This is also called *mujin-engi* (unlimited cause and conditions). This theory unifies appearance and cause and conditions. The important aspects are: All things are the appearance of truth and there is nothing which is separate from the essence of the *Tathagata* (the Truth, Suchness).

Therefore everything is absolute. Even a speck of dust is the appearance of Truth. If everything is absolute, there is nothing else except it. In other words, each and every thing simultaneously includes all other things, like the knots in a net.

All the knots are connected with each other. If you pick up a single knot, you pick up the whole net. This relation is called "*Tai mo ju ju*" (referring to the jewels fastened to the net hanging in Sakra's place which reflect one another endlessly) and "*shu ban mu jin*" (subject-object are inexhaustible).

In other words, the universe is likened to a net of glittering gems, wherein each jewel and its reflection exists in all other gems. There is an interplay of reflections into infinity. In this way a single entity, in contrast to others, becomes the subject, and others become the object. Then when the object becomes the subject; the subject becomes the object. This interplay between subject and object proceeds endlessly. This is called *hokkai-engi*.

Therefore, the temporal relation of cause and conditions leads to the mutual interdependence of differentiated things, which is the spatial relation of cause and effect. In this sense even a particle which cannot be seen with the eye is absolute. This particle contains the entire universe. The entire universe is an object to the particle and is contained within it. This manner of identification (the waves are the water and the water is the waves) and mutual interpenetration (rays of light enter into one another without hindrance) between things are called *jijimuge*. *Jijimuge* means all things and events in the Universe interpenetrate freely without obstruction.

In the final analysis each thing contains everything, and each thing is absolute. Simultaneously each thing is brought into existence by every other thing. This kind of cause and conditions relationship is *hokkai-engi*. This is the highest principle in the theory of cause and conditions.

If we pursue the principle that all things are impermanent and all things flow and change, the temporal principle becomes a spatial principle. At this point, naturally we have come to the question, "What is the spatial principle?" We must pursue the reality of things in a spatial sense and analyze the second truth, *Shoho muga*, the principle that phenomenal things are in existence only by conditions; they have no substance in themselves.

Shoho Muga - Having no Substance in Themselves, all Things Exist only by Conditions

Zen stands on the concrete reality before your eyes. Even so, most people feel that Zen is empty theory separate from concrete reality. This is proof that most people look at life upside down. In reality everything flows, but people think nothing moves. Everything changes, but people think things are permanent. The primary reason for delusions and illusions is the ego [which sees things as existing in themselves]. We want to believe that behind the phenomena we see with our eyes, lies an eternal substance. We are looking for some actual being, original substance, a god, or Buddha which controls the Universe.

As this inquiry progesses, what we looked for outside ourselves, we begin to look for inside ourselves. The result is to think that our original substance is the ego. Because of this, we believe there is an eternal, unchanging, actual being behind the natural universe, and similarly we believe that inside ourselves, there is a solidified, unchanging form which is our center. This we can call the ego.

According to the Upanishad philosophy, the ego is *Jo Itsu Shussai*. *Jo* means always present and never changing. *Itsu* means absolutely one. *Shussai* means mastery of all things. The phrase refers to the actual being or existence which masters all things and is always present and unchanging. This being we call the ego.

Usually we make the ego the center and manage all our affairs from this perspective. Buddha, however, said there is no such thing. He said that the truth is that every phenomenon exists only because of conditions; thus, they have no substance.

Shoho means every phenomenon. We use the term *ho* which means *Dharma* because every phenomenon exists according to the principle of cause and conditions [in contrast to cause and effect. *Dharma* is the principle of cause and conditions]. After all *shoho muga* means all things are interdependent, and there is no thing which exists in itself.

Ji-sho (self-nature) is a Buddhist term; generally the term *jitai* (actual being, substance, or entity) is used instead. This actual being contains the causes of occurrence, continuance, and death or destruction in itself. Because of these causes it occurs, continues, and dies or is destroyed without being influenced from outside itself. If an entity has this kind of force in itself, we call it an actual being. *Muji-sho* (no-self-nature) means that there is no actual being as described above.

Everything we ordinarily experience in this world is interdependent. Reciprocally being cause and conditions of each other, all things create and destroy each other. If cause and conditions match, phenomenon are created. If cause and conditions vanish, phenomenon vanish. This is the fundamental structure of the reality we live in. Namely *shoho jisso* (every phenomenon is itself the ultimate reality) is the true aspect of reality.

There are, however, simple-minded opinions that no-self means that the physical body or the psychological self does not exist. These opinions then contend that if there is no self, how can the world exist? From what I have said, I hope you can see that these opinions are misunderstandings.

According to cause and conditions, the physical elements and mental functioning come together to create what we generally think of as ourselves. In ancient Buddhist terms, the physical body consists of the four material elements of earth, water, fire, and wind. Mental functioning consists of *goun* (Skt. *panca skandha*) (the five aggregates): *shiki-un* (Skt. *rupa-skandha*) (matter or form), *ju-un* (Skt. *vedana-skandha*) (perception), *so-un* (Skt. *samjna-skandha*) (conception), *gyo-un* (Skt. *samskara-skandha*) (volition), and *shiki-un* (Skt. *vijnana-skandha*) (consciousness). Simply put, the physical being cannot be conceived apart from the relationship to the parents which gave it birth or as existing apart from the food and other elements necessary to maintain the body. A self which exists apart from social relationships can be conceived only in the mind and not in reality.

In the mind the self comes into existence at the deepest level which perhaps can be described as wholeness [the level of the storehouse unconscious]. From the connections of the body with the parents and the elements, and the sense of self with historical and societal factors, the self emerges. We can therefore see that there is no actual being; this mutual dependence is what no-self nature means.

In any case the real state of all things or, in other words, the true form of all beings is no-self nature (*mujisho*) and no-self (*muga*). Depending on cause and conditions the true form of all beings changes and flows without stopping. This is certainly true. The real state of all things is formless. This is the meaning of the Tendai philosophy of *kukan*—the meditation on the essential voidness of all existence. The Tendai system of scholarship is based on the contemplation of the void.

In this manner, if you view the world from the perspective of space, it is no-self nature (no fixed nature, nonsubstantiality). If we explain *mujisho* negatively, the true form of all beings is formless, and there is no fixed form. Because all things are formless, rather than saying all things are connected, it is better to say that gods, Buddhas, human beings, animals, and plants, everything is of the same nature and equal. The entire universe is one. However, if we turn this around and explain it positively, because of what I said before, each thing is the true form. That is to say, all things, as they are, are the real state of all things (*shoho jisho*). Everything as they are is the truth. Each one is an absolute being. Nothing has a fixed self. Because there is no fixed self, perhaps we can say each individual entity is the whole. The truth of *shoho muga* reveals the real state of all things.

In this manner, everything in the world we live in has no fixed self. All is formless-form. Because of this real state, each moment or each movement reveals the absolute. Each thing has meaning in existence. [There is nothing which is not needed.] Each thing alone is the absolute being and the World-honored One. Even a maggot in feces is Buddha.

In this manner the real state of all things is formless (*jisso-muso*); this is no-self and non-differentiation. [From the spatial perspective, reality is undifferentiated.] From formlessness and no-self, differentiation appears. The leaves are green, and the flowers are red. This is the perspective of cause and conditions in time.

Initially we began with the temporal principle which in the end changed to the spatial principle. Then we discussed the spatial principle which in the end turned into the temporal principle. [Space and time are one.]

Nehan Jyaku-jo - Nirvana is Tranquility

As I have explained until now, in time cause and conditions perpetually change. I have emphasized differentiation and impermanence. From the spatial perspective the real state of all things is undifferentiated. Both views are right, but this is like separating one drop of water into each element and intellectually understanding the characteristics of hydrogen and oxygen. This abstract knowledge is not a living drop of water.

Because all things are impermanent, everything is uncertain. Because all things depend on conditions, this world is beyond our control. It is feared that these points of view can lead to fatalism. By dividing the single reality into time and space, cause and conditions versus the real state of all things as impermanence and selflessness, you can understand the principles of reality. But these principles are not reality itself. Time is space; space is time. Cause and conditions are the real state; the real state is cause and conditions. Just as hydrogen and oxygen combine to form a living drop of water, these separate principles must be brought together to form a living world.

In this living world, the third truth of the *Dharma*, "*Nirvana* is tranquility," is found at the point where space and time cross. The truth that *Nirvana* is tranquility is not on the same level as the first two truths of the *Dharma*. Rather, when the first two coalesce, *Nirvana* is realized at a higher level.

The Japanese word *nehan* is a translation of the sound of the Sanskrit word *Nirvana*. *Nirvana* means the condition of extinction. It means freedom from the shackles of delusion, the extinction of the delusion of life and death [of all dualism]. *Nirvana* is the state of *satori* (enlightenment). Because of *Nirvana*, the agitation of the mind and emotional suffering disappear. *Jakujo*, therefore, is a condition of stillness in which no waves emerge. *Nehan jakujo* is a world free of the suffering of birth, age, sickness, and death. These four symbolize all suffering in the relative world. In *Nirvana* a person is free from life and death [all dualism], so he lives fully and dies fully in a creative dynamic *samadhi* (*katsu zanmai*).

Because everything is impermanent, we cannot expect anything. Because everything is no-self, nothing goes the way we want. Eventually we may come to believe that this world is fruitless and vain. This mistaken belief arises from an analytic, abstract point of view. It comes about because we are attached to the ego. Then we expect things we cannot expect and want to make things, which do not go our way, to go our way.

If, however, you do not expect things and do not try to make things go your way, even when things do not go your own way, you can find freedom. Even when things you expect to happen do not, you can attain calmness. This is true, isn't it? The world of *Nirvana* is like this: from the perspective of the world of the absolute present, everything is perceived in its suchness without the imposition of the ego. Then the person benefits from and enjoys everything and experiences every day as a fine day.

After all to adhere solely to the view that all things are equal is wrong. To believe only in differentiation as truth is also a fallacy. Equality is differentiation, and differentiation is equality. Emptiness is the wonder of being, and the wonder of being is emptiness. Not one, but not two, this is the [transcendent principle of the] *Dharma* gate. This kind of world is the world of *Nirvana*. In daily life whether moving your hands, raising your feet, coughing, whatever you're doing at that moment, here and now, is *Nirvana*. In the world of *Nirvana*, the whole world can be put in a grain of dust; one movement can easily encompass the whole universe.

Master Rinzai said, "Here in front of my eyes! You, the person listening to my discourse." This person, who can live here and now fully, can live the ultimate and limitless life. This life cannot be grasped as a principle. It must be grasped as an actuality and realized with the body. This is Zen.

The three truths of the *Dharma* are: 1) All things are impermanent. 2) Every phenomenon exists only by conditions. 3) *Nirvana* is tranquility. In the last analysis these three truths of the *Dharma* are actually a single truth of the real state of all things. Provisionally for the purpose of explanation the single truth was divided into three.

Past, present, future—any time must be grasped now in the immediate moment. Spatially any place must be grasped here where you stand. Anyone, old, young, men, or women must be grasped as oneself. This is the principle of the universality of human being. In other words, at the center of the crossing of time and space, this "self" moves. The world of this free activity is the world of *Nirvana*.

This world of *Nirvana* is not separate and far away from the reality here and now in which you live and move. *Nirvana* is not a faraway dream world. It is this very world in which you suffer. Only in the world of *Nirvana* can you experience the end and the means as one, and every day is a fine day. Whatever you do is fulfilling in itself.

Master Hakuin in his "Poisonous Commentary to the Heart *Sutra*" grieves about many people's misunderstanding of ultimate *Nirvana*. They take it to be a calm condition without activity and fall into the pit [of passivity]. This empty, quiet state of no activity is death-like and resembles the life of a ghost. It has less value than rotten socks. Rather than this, Hakuin says, "The birth and destruction of all living things as they are is the *Nirvana* of all Buddhas." Our continuously changing daily lives just as they are in which we laugh, cry, suffer, enjoy, live, and die, are the *Nirvana* of all Buddhas.

Each single movement in our lives is the activity of Tathagata (a name for Buddha which means "one who has come from thusness"). At each moment whatever you are doing or experiencing is genuinely *Nirvana*. This is the world of the absolute present.

The real state of all things, cause and conditions, and equality and differentiation, are like two sides of one reality. They are certainly not separate. If we examine them conceptually, there are two principles, but in reality they are originally one. There is nothing outside of this one reality. The differentiations of each thing are transcended, and differentiation is realized as Oneness. The world of phenomenon as it is is the real state of all things. This kind of world cannot be described, conceived, or explained. This is the world of the absolute present.

Because *Nirvana* cannot be described, conceived, or explained, you must make principle and practice one and *shugyo* (training in the deepest sense) with your body and mind. This is the way of ultimate *Nirvana*. This is Zen. Discarding discriminating knowledge and realizing and expressing the world of the absolute present with the body is Zen.

CHAPTER 7

Zen and the Fine Arts

Along with the Martial Arts and Zen, the fine arts are the third pillar of Omori Roshi's way of training. The martial arts develop power and vitality; Zen develops spiritual insight and depth; and the fine arts develop refinement and aesthetic appreciation. Together they effectively develop a human being who is natural and rounded—two excerpts from Omori Roshi regarding Zen and art follow:

> Zen and the Arts have not only a closely-tied but an inseparable relationship, like Siamese twins. The inseparability arises because Zen absolutely negates the self in the Absolute Being called Buddha and then affirms its Being.
>
> The self once negated is not only the simple limited self but is also the manifestation of Buddha, symbol of that which we revere as Universal Life. When something which cannot be seen or touched is symbolized in this way, it is worthy of recognition as a magnificent work of art. When this occurs, Zen takes the form of artistic expression. But notice, all work from a Zen priest is not necessarily Zen Art. The Art must symbolize the Absolute Void and in the true religious sense Zen Art must symbolize Buddha Mind.
>
> From ancient times, the traditional arts of Japan were created by immersing oneself into an object (the dualism of self and object is transcended). Thus the one creating is also the creation and thereby contains the fundamental characteristics of Japanese culture: *wabi* and *sabi*. *Wabi* means that an object, though still a part of everyday society, stands apart from it in solitude. *Sabi* connotes simple, rustic imperfection without decorations. For example, a painting showing extremely few strokes manifests *sabi* or omission.
>
> These unique characteristics of Japanese culture were brought about by Zen. Zen artworks represent simplicity, bottomless depth and profundity. *Yugen* (that which gives a glimpse into the Unfathomable) was born. Zen Art is the unrestrained work of one who creates freely as one's will dictates.[1]

In the real world of *yuge zammai* (the play of *samadhi*), the Zen of the True Man without Rank (Rinzai's term for the True Self) is vibrant with life. Because this is the basis of whatever the Zen master draws, everything is a magnificent work of Zen art. Even when a Zen artist has mastered Zen, he cannot completely disregard technique, however. Needless to say, when he does an artwork, technique must naturally work with his Zen realization. No matter how much he has mastered Zen, if he has never practiced calligraphy, it is impossible to draw *bokuseki* (calligraphy by a Zen master). Without holding a brush even once, he cannot create a magnificent ink painting. This would be like letting Hakuin (perhaps the greatest Japanese Rinzai Zen master) pilot a jet plane. He cannot do it no matter how great a Zen master he is. Even if you have high spiritual attainment, you obviously cannot use techniques unless you are skilled in them. On the other hand, even if you master techniques completely, it makes you only a skilled technician of calligraphy or painting.

For Zen art, it is of primary importance to strongly grasp your True Self and to realize the great light and power of the absolute freedom which transcends all restrictions. If this is lacking, one cannot create art which will move the spirit of people. Additionally, you must have the technique which can fully express this great light and power. Otherwise, you cannot attain the highest levels of art. If you ask whether self-realization or technique is more fundamental, understand that the True Man without Rank is fundamental, and technique is an outgrowth of the True Man without Rank.[2]

While Omori Roshi's comments above pertain to the relationship between Zen and the arts generally, in practice Omori Roshi's art was calligraphy. He and Yokoyama Setsudo founded a school of calligraphy called *Hitsuzendo* which integrates the Jubokudo style of calligraphy with the *kiai* of the *Hojo*. Omori Roshi explains:

> *Hitsu* is the brush that absorbs and projects the practitioner's state of mind; *zen* is to function wholeheartedly in the present time and place, free of all smallness of mind; and *do* is the Way of continuous practice. Unity of all three elements must be attained.[3]

Hitsuzendo complements both Zen and the martial arts training as it provides a lasting record of one's level of insight at any given time. It also cultivates an appreciation of aesthetic relationships between space, time, and energy, and develops intuitive perception as one learns to see the practitioner's personality within his line. The practice of *Hitsuzendo* begins with the drawing of *mujibo* (a single straight line). Omori Roshi explains the significance of this simple act:

> Whatever is present in the practitioner's mind will be present in the *mujibo*; unless there is a total dedication and hard training, a real line will never appear on paper. A *mujibo* is like a decisive cut of a live sword in a fight to the finish; it slices the Universe in two. If anything is held back, there can be no *mujibo*. One calligraphy master in the past refused to acknowledge anyone as his student who was not drenched with sweat after writing one *mujibo*.[4]

Drawing just one line well requires the practitioner to throw himself entirely into each moment, that is, into each dot which makes up the line. For *kiai* to flow freely and deeply, the tip of the brush must move from the *hara* without interference from conscious thought or unnatural tensions in the body.

Rather than elements of form or composition, the essence of *Hitsuzendo* is *bokki*, the *kiai* the calligrapher transmits to the ink particles. This energy penetrates the paper and has been termed "eternal energy" because it can be felt in calligraphy that are centuries old.

Omori Roshi doing Hitsuzendo during sesshin *at Farrington High School, Honolulu (c. 1974).*

Bokki is a subtle quality perhaps best described as the depth and shine of a line. It does not depend on the color of the ink or the excellence of the brush and paper. Viewed under an electron microscope in a line with vibrant *bokki*, the ink dots are all aligned. *Bokki* depends on *ki*, the vital energy or spiritual power the practitioner transmits. Omori Roshi explains:

> The clarity of the *bokki*, the *ki* in the ink, indicates the level of insight. *Bokki* is not only seen with the eyes; it is sensed with the *hara*, the physical and spiritual center of one's body. *Bokki* reveals the calligrapher's inner light. *Bokki* is not identical to the brushstroke, but it is not independent either. It cannot be dissected or arranged into neat compartments. When a Zen calligrapher pours his or her spirit into each stroke, every line becomes a vibrant force. Zen is the art of *kiai*.[5]

As in the martial arts, *kiai* is generated through breathing, the use of the *hara*, and intense concentration. As a person brushes a line, his or her breath must be smooth and even or the line will be broken and jagged. The movement of the brush must originate from the *hara* and not the arm and hand. Concentration must be as intense as if engaged in a life and death encounter.

Kiai can be experienced but not defined. It is sensed through an intuitive perception involving the workings of both consciousness and the *hara*, the physical and spiritual center of being in the lower abdomen. A work of art, whether it be a swordcut in *Kendo*, a bowl in ceramics, or a brushstroke in calligraphy, must radiate *kiai* to be considered Zen art.

To experience *bokki* clearly, original works of art should be viewed, but perhaps the following works of Omori Roshi can convey a sense of his art and spirit.

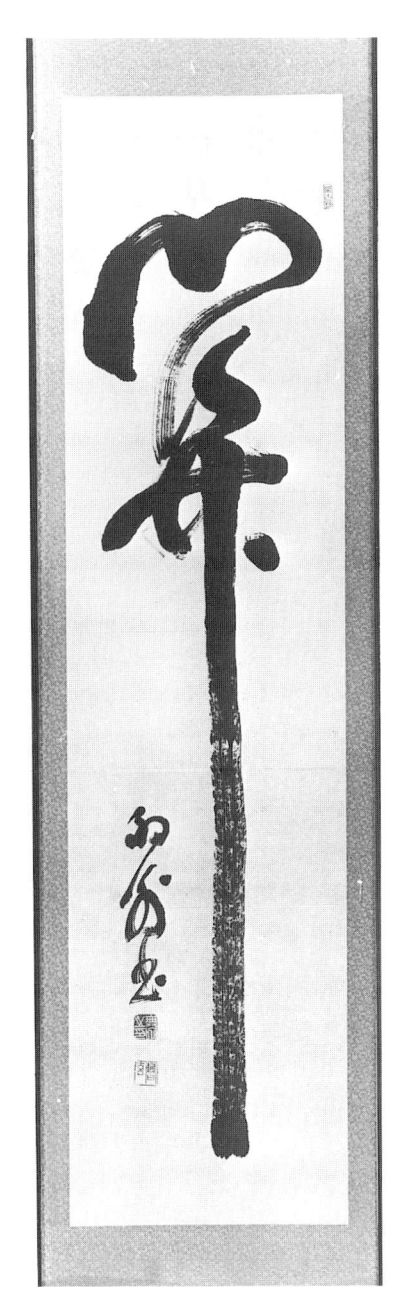

Kan - *Barrier, Impassable.*

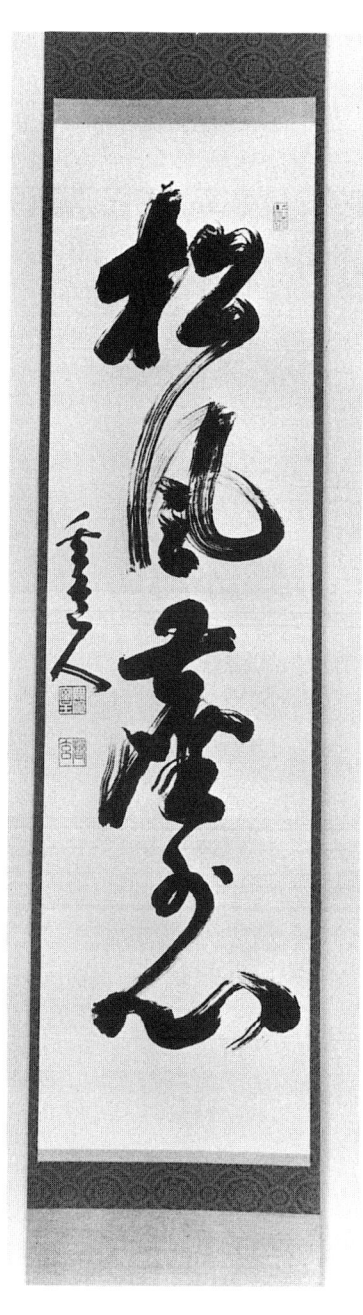

Shofu jingai no shin - *Wind through the pine trees; heart free of the dust of this world.*

Zuisho ni shu to naru - *Make yourself master everywhere.*

Appendices

Books by Omori Sogen

With the exception of *An Introduction to Zen Training* (1996) and *Zen and Budo* (1989), all of the following books are in the Japanese language. A translation of their title is shown in parentheses.

Nihonteki Sekai no Keisei (Creating a Japanese-style World). Aichi Prefecture: Kodo-juku, 1942.

Shibu no Roku Kun Chu (Comments and Notes for Four Zen Texts). Kyoto: Kichu-jo, 1962.

Rinzai-roku Shinko (Commentaries on *The Record of Lin-chi*). Aichi Prefecture: Reimei-shobo, 1964.

Sanzen Nyumon (An Introduction to Zen Training). Tokyo: Shunjyu-sha, 1964.

Ken to Zen (Swordsmanship and Zen). Tokyo: Shunjyu-sha, 1966.

Sho to Zen (Calligraphy and Zen). Tokyo: Shunjyu-sha, 1966.

Zen o Ikiru (Living by Zen). Tokyo: Hayashi-shoten, 1967.

Zen no Shinzui (The Essence of Zen). Tokyo: Kyoiku-shincho-sha, 1967.

Yamaoka Tesshu (A Life of Yamaoka Tesshu). Tokyo: Shunjyu-sha, 1968.

Shingan (The Mind's Eye). Tokyo: Hakujyu-sha, 1968.

Zen no Michi (The Way of Zen). Tokyo: Seishin-shobo, 1971.

Zuisho ni Shu to Naru (Make Yourself the Master of Every Situation). Aichi Prefecture: Reimei-shobo, 1972.

Hekigan Roku 1 & 2 (Commentaries on *The Blue Cliff Record 1 & 2*). Tokyo: Hakujyu-sha, 1976.

Yuima Kyo Nyumon (An Introduction to *The Vimalakirtinirdesha Sutra*). Tokyo: Hakujyu-sha, 1977.

Hito no Ueni Tatsu Hito no Kokoro (The Spirit of Leadership). Tokyo: Nihon-jitsugyo-shuppan-sha, 1978.

Zen no Koso (A Short Biography of Japanese Zen Masters). Tokyo: Shujyu-sha, 1979.

Hannya Shingyo Kowa (Commentaries on *The Hannya-haramitta Sutra*). Tokyo: Hakujyu-sha, 1981.

Dokugyo Chu Shingyo (Commentaries on Zen Master Hakuin's *Shingyo Sutra*). Tokyo: Shujyu-sha, 1981.

Rinzai-roku Kowa (Commentaries on *The Record of Lin-chi*). Tokyo: Shunjyu-sha, 1983.

Zen no Ha'so (The Idea of Zen). Tokyo: Kodan-sha, 1983.

Jyugyu Zu (Commentaries on *The Ten Ox-herding Pictures*). Tokyo: Hakujyu-sha, 1983.

Sanzen Nyumon (An Introduction to Zen Training - pocket-book series). Tokyo: Kodan-sha, 1986.

Roankyo Kowa (Commentaries on the Teachings of Zen Master Suzuki Shozan). Tokyo: Daihorin-kaku, 1986.

Zen and Budo (trans. of Zen to Budo). Honolulu: Daihonzan Chozen-ji, 1989.

An Introduction to Zen Training (trans. of *Sanzen Nyumon*). London: Kegan Paul International, 1996.

Endnotes

NOTE: If an author is not given, the work is by Omori Sogen.

Chapter 1 - Shugyo: 1904–1934

[1] *Te'shu*, Vol. 104, a monthly magazine published by Te'shu-kai, Tokyo.
[2] as told to Hosokawa Dogen by Omori Sogen.
[3] *Roan-kyo Ko-wa*.
[4] material from *Te'shu*, Vol. 98; *Shingan*; and *Roankyo Kowa*.
[5] the word *hara* when used in a physical sense relates to the region of the lower abdomen.
[6] *Te'shu*, Vol. 99.
[7] *Zen Bun-ka*, Vol. 91, a quarterly magazine published by the Institute for Zen Studies, Kyoto.
[8] material from *Te'shu*, Vol. 106, and *Roankyo Kowa*.
[9] material from *Te'shu*, Vol. 107, and *Shingan*.
[10] material from *Te'shu*, Vol. 119, and *Roankyo Kowa*.
[11] material from *Te'shu*, Vols. 113, 114 and 115; *Roankyo Kowa*; and *Hito no Ueni Tatsu Hito no Kokoro*.
[12] material from *Zen Bun-ka*, Vol. 91; *Shingan*; and *Roankyo Kowa*.
[13] *Te'shite Ikiru*. published by Kosei shu'pan. 1976.
[14] material from *Roankyo Kowa* and as told by Omori Roshi.
[15] material from *Te'shu*, Vols. 102 and 103.
[16] material from *Te'shu*, Vols. 137 and 192; *Roankyo Kowa*; and *Sho to Zen*.
[17] from *Zen Bun-ka*, Vol. 91.
[18] Daisetz T. Suzuki, *Zen and Japanese Culture* (Princeton: Princeton University Press, 1970), 109.
[19] Suzuki, *Zen and Japanese Culture*, 157.
[20] Suzuki, *Zen and Japanese Culture*, 178.

Chapter 2 - Renma: 1934–1945

[1] material from *Te'shu*, Vol. 110.
[2] material from *Te'shu*, Vols. 109, 113, and 119; *Roankyo Kowa*.
[3] material from *Roankyo Kowa*.
[4] material from *Roankyo Kowa*.

[5] material from *Te'shu*, Vol. 192; *Roankyo Kowa*.
[6] *Ga-o Roshi I-kun*, published by Tenryu-ji, Kyoto, 1957.
[7] material from *Roankyo Kowa*.

Chapter 3 - Gogo no Shugyo: 1945–1994

[1] Jiun Sonja (1718–1804), a famous priest of Japanese Shingon Buddhism.
[2] material from *Roankyo Kowa*.
[3] material from *Roankyo Kowa* and Hito no Ueni Tatsu Hito no Kokoro.
[4] material from *Roankyo Kowa* and Hito no Ueni Tatsu Hito no Kokoro.
[5] Hito no Ueni Tatsu Hito no Kokoro.
[6] material from *Roankyo Kowa*.
[7] material from *Shingan*.
[8] material from *Te'shu*, Vol. 108.
[9] material from *Rinzai-roku Shinko*.
[10] material from *Roankyo Kowa* and *Te'shu*, Vol. 133.
[11] Yuan-wu K'o-ch'in, Pi-Yen Lu (Jpn. *Hekigan Roku*) (The Blue Cliff Record) (12th century). This famous Chinese Zen text is composed of a series of one hundred lectures given by Yuan-we K'o-ch'in (1063– 1135), a famous master in the 4th generation of the Yang-Ch'i line of Lin-Chi (Rinzai) Zen.
[12] Suzuki Shosan, *Roankyo* (Donkey-Saddle Bridge) Collected by Echu, 1660.
[13] *Shido Bunan Zenji Kana Hogo* (The Sayings of Zen Master Shindo Bunan Zenji) (Edo: Edo Matsu-kai, 1671).
[14] material from *Roankyo Kowa*.
[15] Dogen Zenji, *Shobo-genzo* (Treasure Chamber of the Eye of True Dharma) (Publisher and date unknown).

Chapter 4 - Zen and Budo

[1] The character *Bu* is composed of the characters for "stop" and "spear;" thus, *Bu* refers to martial or military matters. The character *Do* is the same as the *Tao* (the Way).
[2] This chapter is a translation of *Zen to Budo*, an essay by Omori Roshi that was first published in Japan, Daisetz T. Suzuki and Nishitani, eds., Zen, Vol. 5, *Zen and Culture* (Chikuma Shobo, 1968). A more formal translation has already been published, Omori Sogen, *Zen and Budo*, trans. Tenshin

Tanouye (Honolulu: Daihonzan Chozen-ji/ International Zen Dojo, 1989).

[3] Nakae Toju founded the Japanese line of the Confucianism of Wang Yang-ming. Wang Yang-ming (1472-1529) was a philosopher, scholar, incorruptible high government official and a brilliant general who won his campaigns with a minimum of bloodshed. In Japan (where his name is read as O Yomei), his doctrines were very influential.

[4] The duties of the Five Relations are incumbent on all, and there are three virtues for their practice. The Relations are: sovereign-subject, parent-child, elder brother-younger brother, master-servant, and friend-friend. The three virtues are knowledge, magnanimity, and vigor. According to Confucius in his *Doctrine of the Mean* (XX.8), these must be practiced single-mindedly.

[5] This is the Way of Giving Life (*ikasu*) in which the lowest level shows correct use, the next levels shows creative use, and the final level shows godly use.

[6] "Buddha" here stands for Life, Consciousness, Whole, Void.

[7] Editor's note: this is a particularly difficult paragraph to translate. First, recall that this essay was written in 1968 during the active phase of the Cold War. Secondly, the penultimate sentence of the paragraph is based on a famous saying from swordsmanship: My opponent cuts my skin, I cut his flesh. He cuts my flesh, I cut his bone. He cuts my bone, I kill him. Omori Roshi is saying that, although the Superpowers find themselves in the posture of kill or be killed, this posture can be transcended into ainuke, a mutual recognition that no fight is possible.

Chapter 5 - Practical Zen

[1] material from *Te'shite Ikiru*.

[2] Suzuki Shosan, *Roankyo*.

[3] Bodhidharma. (Chin. P'u-ti-ta-mo). (Jpn. Bodaidaruma or Daruma). 470–543. The first Chinese patriarch of Zen.

[4] Hui-neng, Chinese Zen Master. 638–713. (Jpn. Eno).

[5] Philip Yampolsky, trans. *The Platform Sutra of the Sixth Patriarch* (New York: Columbia University Press, 1967), 140.

[6] Yampolsky, *The Platform Sutra of the Sixth Patriarch*, 137-138.

[7] Hung-jen, Chinese Zen Master. 601–674. (Jpn. Gunin).

[8] Shen-hsiu, Chinese Zen Master. 605?–706. (Jpn. Jinshu).

[9] material from *Roankyo Kowa*.

[10] Nio Zen. (Jpn.) Suzuki Shosan was an advocate of a vigorous form of Zen named after the two Nio, or deities, that guard the entrance to Buddhist temples.

[11] material from *Te'shite Ikiru*.
[12] Hui-K'o, Chinese Zen Master. 487–593. (Jpn. Eka).
[13] This translation combines Daisetz T. Suzuki, *Essays in Zen Buddhism*, First Series (New York: Grove Press, 1961), 190, and Zenkei Shibayama, *Zen Comments on the Mumonkan*, trans. Kudo (New York: Harper and Row, 1974), 285.
[14] Tao-hsuan, *Ching-te ch'uan-teng-lu* (Jpn. Keitoku Dento-roku) (*The Record of the Transmission of Light*) (11th century).
[15] Nan-yueh Hai-jang, Chinese Zen Master. 677-744. (Jpn. Nangaku Ejo).
[16] Yuan-wu Ko-ch'in, Chinese Zen Master. 1063-1135. (Jpn. Engo Kokugon).
[17] Ta-hui Tsung-kao, Chinese Zen Master. 1089-1163. (Jpn. Daie Soko).
[18] Chao-chou, Chinese Zen Master. 778-897. (Jpn. Joshu).
[19] Wu-men Hui-k'ai, *Wu-men-kuan* (Jpn. *Mumonkan*) (The Gateless Gate), one of the most important *koan* collections in Zen literature.
[20] Wu-men Hui-k'ai, Chinese Zen Master. 1183–1260. (Jpn. Mumon Ekai).
[21] Shibayama, *Zen Comments on the Mumonkan*, 19-20.
[22] Negating everything means to attain absolute *samadhi*. Reaffirming everything is to break through this state and realize Everything-in-its-isness.
[23] material from *Roankyo Kowa*.
[24] material from *Roankyo Kowa*.
[25] At the age of 75, even when I thought he was a great Zen master beyond comparison with others, Omori Roshi told me, "Before I die, I want to have just one day of the continuation of right concentration."
[26] material from *Roankyo Kowa*.
[27] San-sheng Hui-jan, comp., *Lin-chi Lu* (Jpn. *Rinzai Roku*) (*Record of the Words of Lin-chi*) (Ninth century).
[28] material from *Te'shite Ikiru*.
[29] material from *Roankyo Kowa*.

Chapter 6 - *Teisho*: The World of the Absolute Present

[1] Shibayama, *Zen Comments on the Mumonkan*, 58.
[2] Hui-wen, Chinese Zen Master. (no dates). (Jpn. Emon).
[3] Gokan-engi (Skt. karma). Universal law of cause and effect—all phenomena and things in this world occur by karma of all beings.

Arayashiki-engi (Skt. alaya-vijana). Central notion of the Yogachara School of the Mahayana sect, which sees storehouse consciousness, the basic consciousness of everything existing—the essence of the world, out of which everything that is, arises. This theory is based on Gokan-engi. The "seed" of arayashiki-engi is the cause of all phenomena and things.

Shinnyo-engi (Skt. tathata). According to the Mahayana Buddhist teaching, all beings have Buddha Nature. This theory describes the relationship between our worldly desires and Buddha Nature.

Hokkai-engi (Skt. Dharma-dhatu). The realm of the Dharma. All things interpenetrate each other and exist without any hindrance. They do not exist independently. Therefore, the cause/condition/effect of all phenomena and things are affected by each other. This theory is one of the key concepts of the Kegon school of Buddhism.

Chapter 7 - Zen and the Fine Arts

[1] material from *Zen to Gei-jyutsu* (Zen and the Arts).

[2] material from *Sho to Zen*.

[3] Omori Sogen and Terayama Katsujo, *Zen and the Art of Calligraphy*, trans. John Stevens (New York: Routledge and Kegan Paul, 1983), 89.

[4] Omori and Terayama, *Zen and the Art of Calligraphy*, 94.

[5] Omori and Terayama, *Zen and the Art of Calligraphy*, 10.

Index

Absolute Being, 154
adversity, 66
aesthetic appreciation, 154
Aikido, 103
ainuke (mutual passing), 72-73, 110-111; Harigaya Sekiun, 72; transcending dualism, 73
aiuchi (mutual killing), 109-110, 114; to master *ainuke*, 73
animal instincts, 107
arrest, during Army Officers Revolt, 45
arts, significance to training, 42
Asakusa Kannon, 112
Atsumi Masaru, spirit of cutting through difficulty, 31; touring with, 30-31
attachment, to the ego, 113; to thoughts, 118
Bankei Zenji, 80, 99
barrier, reaching one's limit, 126, 128
becoming one with, 131
Bodhidharma, 118-119, 124
Bodhisattva Kannon, 112
bokki, 156, 158
Book of Five Rings, 108
breath, 120, 122; and *kiryoku*, 121-122, 158; counting, 122
bu (chivalry, martial arts), 102-103, 112
Buddha Mind, 154
Buddha, 91, 124-125, 136-137, 146, 152
Buddhist law, 137
Buddhist theory, 137-138, 144

Budo, 114; definition of, 102; mistaken aim of, 102, 108; Way of Tao, 102-103
bugei (martial arts), 102
bujutsu (combat techniques), 102
bun (culture, civilization, "letters"), 102-103
bundo, 112
bushi (warrior), 102
Bushido (Way of Samurai), 43, 106, 111
calligraphy, 155; developing an "eye" for, 36; *mujibo* (single straight line of calligraphy), 156
cause and conditions, 142, 144
center of being, 158
center of the universe, 66, 125
character, as developed by criticism, 92; as shown by cleaning, 86
chikusho heiho (beastly fighting), 107-109
Chozen-ji/International Zen Dojo, canon, 95; establishment of, 81-82
compassion, 135-136
concentration, 158
conditions, *see* cause and conditions.
Confucian relationships, 103
consciousness, like *juzu* (Buddhist rosary), 121; of the unconscious, 71
culture, *see bun*
Daie Soko (Ta-hui Tsung-kao), 124
Daisetz Suzuki, in Hawaii, 78; on *shugyo*, 37-38; regard for *Ken to Zen*, 71

Appendices 171

Daito Kokushi, 65
delusion, 133, 146
Dharma gate, 151
Dharma, 150; definition of, 146; three truths of, 151
Dogen Zenji, 43, 98, 111, 133
Doing-nothing-time, 131
Dotoku (Tao-teh), 103
doubt, mass of, 126-128
dualism, 73, 111, 150, 154; as the original sin, 107; between killing and giving life, 110
ecology, 92
ego, 38, 92, 146, 150; used to transcend ego, 113; Zen negation of, 113
Eka, 123
Emperor, restoration of, 45
emptiness, 134, 137, 151
engiron, see cause and conditions.
Engo Kokugon (Yuan-wu Ko-ch'in), 124
enlightenment, 28, 125-127; achieving, 134; Eno's explanation of, 118; living according to true self-nature, 105; three necessities for, 133; through counting breaths, 120-121; through sutra, 130
Eno, 119-120
every day is a fine day, 151-152
evolution, 106
existence, as an individual, 92; in Buddhism, 136; in relation, 146
expectations, 66, 150
Farrington High School, 79
fatalism, 149
fearlessness, gift of, 112
February Incident, 45
fine arts, 154
five senses, 119
formlessness, 149

Fount of East-West Culture, 95
freedom, 127
gan (glare, stare), 113
Garland Sutra, 136
General Araki, 40-41
Great Life, 43
Great Vehicle, 58
Gudo Toshoku Zenji, 128
Gunin, (Hung-jen), 119
Hagakure, 106, 111
Hakko Ichiu (universal brotherhood), 53-54
Hakuin, 122, 126, 130-131, 152, 155
Hamachi Hachiro, 130
Hanazono University, president of, 88; professor at, 76
hara, 9, 176
Harigaya Sekiun, 109-110; and *ainuke*, 72
Hekigan Roku, 124
Hitsuzendo (Way of the Brush), 131-132, 155-156; beginnings of, 34
Hojo, 13-15, 155; and ki, 14; demonstrating in Europe, 95; demonstration for Tanouye Roshi, 80-81; four seasons, 13-14; Matsumoto Bizen no Kami Naokatsu, 13; one-hundred-times practice, 14, 26
human existence, nature of, 114; structure of, 105-107
illusion, 146
Immovable Wisdom, 109
Imoto Saburo Yoshiaki, 4
Imperial Proclamation, 59
inka, 138
interdependence, 143
interpenetration, *see jijimuge*
intuitive perception, *see kan*
Japanese Buddhist League, 76
Japanese Red Army, 77
jijimuge (interpenetration without

172

obstruction), 145
jikijitsu (head monk), 127
Jikishin Dojo, 41; daily routine at, 42; dissolution of, 54; headquarters of People's Movement, 45; Kuroki Shosa, 41; role of Toyama Mitsuru, 42; role of Toyama Ryusuke, 41-42
Jikishin Kage School, 10-11
Joshu (Chao-chou), 124
Judo, 103-104; decision to study, 13; Kano Jigoro, 104
Kadowaki Kakichi, 95
kaido, 84
Kaisan Rekijyu Tenryu Tekio Osho Daizenji, 98
kalpa, 163
kan (intuitive perception), 80, 156, 158-159.
Kanemaru Sotetsu, 81
Kano Jigoro, 104
Kegon School (Chi Hua-yen), 91, 142
keiko, 37
Keio University, 79
Ken to Zen, 71, 79, 105
Kendo, 9, 79, 103-104; 24-hour training, 11; *ainuke*, 72; as work of art, 158; beginning of, 4; death of, 104; *men*, 11; samadhi, 116; zazen, 116
kensho, definition of, 118
ki, 156, 158
kiai, 80, 155-158; and zazen, 120, 133
kiryoku (vital energy), 121-122
knowledge, 142, 149
koan, 125; a dog's Buddha nature, 124; and other activities, 123; and zazen, 123; answer to, 124-125; becoming one with, 134; before your parents were born, 126; beginning of, 123; break through, 28; definition of, 122; enlightenment, 127; how to *kufu*, 123-124; how to pacify the mind, 123; *Kofu no Antoku*, 122; method to solve, 124; mirror, 135; *mu*, 120-121, 125; *samadhi*, 128; *sanzen*, 124; *satori*, 134; sound of one hand clapping, 126; what walked here, 123
Koho-in, 59, 69, 96; home to Yamaoka Tesshu, 59; property dispute, 61; Seisetsu Roshi's retreat, 59
kokoro (mind, heart), 112
Konoe Cabinet, 50
Konoe Fumimaro, and Manchurian Incident, 19
Konoe, refusal to get Imperial Mandate, 51-52
kufu (to strive or wrestle with), 37, 123
kunren, 37
Kuroki Shosa, and the Jikishin Dojo, 41
Lawyer's Study Group, 69
lay person, 132
Lectures on the Record of the Rinzai, 74
life and death, 150
Lotus Sutra, 128
Maeda Torao, Shinpei Incident, 40
Maeno Jisui, 4-8
magistrate, 69
Maha Kasho, 140
make yourself master everywhere, 161
Mamiya Eiju, 127
Man, 93, 106; as center of the universe, 92-93; negation of, 111; survival of the fittest, 107-109

Manchurian Incident, 40
marriage, 47
Martial Arts, 154; and Way for Man, 104-105; difference from sports, 106
Martial Ways, 43, 103-104, 106
Matsumoto Bizen no Kami Naokatsu, 13
mediation, 71
Michel Foucault, 89-90
Middle Way, 142
mind and body, 152; unity of, 125
Miyamoto Musashi, 95, 107-108, 111, 113; and arts, 110; enlightenment of, 108; *Gorin no Sho*, 108; immovable wisdom, 109; *myoki* (wonderous play), 110; principle of the Way, 108; *shugyo*, 108; swordsmanship, 109
monastery, 127
money, borrowing, 65
mu, as a koan, 24, 30; transcendance of, 125-127
Mujushinken Ryu (School of Non-Abiding Mind), *see* Harigaya Sekiun
Mumon Ekai (Wu-men Hui-k'ai), 124-125
Mumonkan, 124
munen muso (no thought), 133
mutual dependence, 148
mutual passing, *see ainuke*
myoki (wonderous play), 110
Myoshin-ji, 78
myoyo (use of the wonderous), 110
Nakae Toju, *Bun Bu Mondo*, 112; *Okina Mondo*, 102-103
Nakayama Hakudo, 4
Nangaku Ejo, 123
Nansobo, 128-129
Nanton School, 119

Nanzen-ji, 84-85
nature and Man, 92
nehan, see Nirvana
New Japan Anti-Communist League, 69
Nguyen Kao Ky, 74
Nio Zen, 122
Nishida Kitaro, 58
no-form, 118
no-mind, 113
no-self (*muga*), 113, 147
no-thought, 118
nothingness, mistaken view of, 137
now, absolute, 131
nuclear arms, 105, 114
Oda Sensei, 8-9
Omori Sogen, change of name, 4; death of mother, 5; enlightenment experience, 28; lectures, 77; public funeral, 97-99; typical schedule, 87
one-hundred-times practice, *see hyappon keiko*
oneness (*ichinyo*), 129, 152
Onishi Hidetaka, 14
Original Nature, 91
peace, 105-107; peace activists, 114
physical experience and theory, 92
space-being, 141
spiritual exchange to Europe, 95
spiritual poverty, 64
suchness, *see* Tathagata
suffering, 66-67, 150, 152; doing the right thing, 61-66; grabbing at straws, 63; sinking to the bottom, 63; spirit becoming impoverished, 63
Sumo Digest, 86
sutra, 138; how to read, 128-129
Suzuki Shozan, awakening thoughts, 114; *Roankyo*, 114, 117, 121

sword that "gives life," 114
swordsmanship, 109
tanden, 121-122, 129, 133
Tanouye Tenshin, 78-82; *inka shomei* from Omori Roshi, 82; meeting Omori Roshi, 78; request of Omori Roshi, 80-81
tanren, 37
Tathagata, 152
Tendai School, 91, 142, 148
Tenryu-ji, Archbishop of, 84; commuting to, 64; entering priesthoood, 58; role in funeral, 97; Seki Bokuo, 56
The Logic of Listening, 69
Thich Quang Duc, 74-76
three truths of Buddhism, 142
time and space, 142
time, 143-144, 150
time-being, 141
Toji-in, 54
Toyama Mitsuru, 15-16; advice, 61; and the *yakuza*, 15; Black Dragon Society, 15; Dark Ocean Society, 15
Toyama Motokazu, 79
Toyama Ryusuke, 15, 17; anger of, 19; compassion of, 19; death of, 22; Diamond Sutra, 21; Manchurian Incident, 19; Sasaki Moko-o, 18; *se mu i sha* (giver of fearlessness), 22; tuberculosis, 19-20; will power, 21
training, 132-134; after realization, 137; Dharma principle, 140; enlightenment, 137; Entrance by Conduct, 136-138; Entrance by Reason, 136-138; finishing, 138; more than one lifetime, 138
tranquility, *see Nirvana*
transcending Life and Death, 111

Trevor Leggett, 95
Triple Alliance, 45
true Buddha life, 99
True Man without Rank, 74
True Nature, 119
True Self, 111, 126-128, 140, 155; and *kensho*, 118; through exhaling, 121
Tsukahara Bokuden, 80
uncertainty, 149
Unfathomable, *see yugen*
Universal Brotherhood, 53
Universal Life, 154
universe, the natural, 146
Upanishad philosophy, 146
Vietnam, Ambassador Emerson, 75; visit to, 74
vital energy, *see kiryoku*
Void, 154
wabi, 154
Way for Man, 104, 106
Way of swordsmanship, 112-114
Way of the *Samurai, see Bushido*
wisdom, 135
wisdom-compassion, 135
world of phenomenon, 152
World of Play, 107-111
World War II, 48-51; attempt to prevent Japan's involvement, 48-50; Emperor's decision to end, 59; obstructing Emperor's broadcast, 51; Yokoyama Sensei, 51-52
Yagyu Sekishusai, 95
Yamada Ittokusai, *Nippon Kendo-shi*, (History of Japanese *Kendo*), 102, 104, 108; on Musashi, 107, 109
Yamada Jirokichi, 9-11, 36
Yamada Mumon Roshi, 28, 88
Yamaoka Tesshu, 111-113, 138

Appendices

Yokoyama Setsudo, 155; 3-incense zazen, 33; critique of Zen priest calligraphy, 36; Japanese calligraphy, 16-17, 32, 36; mountain cave at Mt. Akagi, 34; *seppuku*, 51-52; teacher of, 33; teaching singing, 34-35

Yoshie Yamashita, 47

yugen, 154

Zazen Club, 78

zazen, 114, 120-122, 127; and delusions, 133; and *kiai*, 121; definition of, 118; different methods of, 116; essence of, 116; everything becomes zazen, 36-37; meaning of working zazen, 133; non-sitting form of, 137; transmission from India to China, 117; valorous mind, 26; while holding sword, 116

Zen and Swordsmanship, *see Ken to Zen*

Zen and Western People, 90-91

Zen, and the Ways, 104-105; art, 154, 158; Chinese influence on, 118; contribution to modern society, 90; different activities, 116; dynamic, 120; goal of, 132; historical development of, 119-120; method of, 126; philosophy of, 119; realization, 155; realized with body, 151; relationship to art, 154; training, 116-120, 154